MW00653962

Praise for *How to Be a Power Connector*

"If you've ever wanted to get to the true core of successful networking without all of the fluff, from an Expert above all 'experts,' look no further than Judy's brilliant approach born out of her own incredible accomplishments by living what she speaks. I can truly say that in my own career of networking and knowing others who preach it, not even one of them comes close to Judy's insight, married with relentless practice, and has more results to show for it than all of the others combined. This book wins the Oscar as the best one out there!"

—Mike Muhney, cofounder of ACT! and
CEO and cofounder of VIPorbit

"I love the power and synergy of connecting and know that once you pick up this book and experience the know-how Judy Robinett has shared within its pages for being a true super connector ... you won't want to put it down. *How to Be a Power Connector* is an absolute must-read."

—Kevin Hall, international bestselling author of *Aspire:
Discovering Your Purpose Through the Power of Words*

"Judy Robinett has written the definitive guide on how to connect with people and develop your contacts into strategic relationships that are both meaningful and profitable. You will never look at meeting someone new the same way again!"

—Kathy Zader, president of Go-Givers International

"Judy Robinett is amazing—with one e-mail or phone call she can put you in touch with anyone you need to know. In *How to Be a Power Connector*, she lays out a foolproof system for finding and connecting with people who can help you, and deepening those relationships by adding value. It's the ultimate shortcut to success—I wish I'd had this book at the beginning of my career!"

—Mark Burnett, executive producer of
Shark Tank, *The Apprentice*, and *Survivor*

How to Be a
POWER
CONNECTOR

The
5+50+100 RULE

for Turning Your
Business Network
into Profits

JUDY ROBINETT

New York Chicago San Francisco Athens London
Madrid Mexico City Milan New Delhi
Singapore Sydney Toronto

1 2 3 4 5 6 7 8 9 0   DOC/DOC   1 2 0 9 8 7 6 5 4

ISBN   978-0-07-183073-7
MHID   0-07-183073-1

e-ISBN   978-0-07-183074-4
e-MHID   0-07-183074-X

Library of Congress Cataloging-in-Publication Data

Robinett, Judy.
    How to be a power connector : the 5+50+100 rule for turning your business network into profits / by Judy Robinett.
        pages cm
    ISBN-13: 978-0-07-183073-7 (hardback)
    ISBN-10: 0-07-183073-1 (hardback)
    1. Business networks. 2. Strategic alliances (Business) 3. Social media. I. Title.
    HD69.S8R633 2014
    658'.044—dc23   2014001655

McGraw-Hill Education books are available at special quantity discounts to use as premiums and sales promotions or for use in corporate training programs. To contact a representative, please visit the Contact Us pages at www.mhprofessional.com.

To all of my friends, family, and foes,
for their love, support, and wisdom.

Contents

Foreword

Harvard Business School (where I received my MBA) is all about network-ing and connecting people—but I never enjoyed that part of my time there. I'm not the most outgoing person in the world, nor am I the "life of the party"; the thought of going to a cocktail party or networking event with people I didn't know was painful. But the other reason I used to find net-working so difficult was that my concept was flawed. Most people approach networking with a very specific purpose in mind: to reach someone they need to know. But that's a superficial view. Building a network isn't simply exchanging business cards and eventually picking up the phone and calling people when you need them. Today I think of networking as *getting to know people that I enjoy and genuinely taking an interest in them.*

I didn't really learn about the power of a network until I started running a start-up business called Skullcandy. There I quickly discovered that every-thing we accomplished happened through other people, through a team, and through a network. Whether it was being able to pick up the phone and say, "I need to reach the CMO of Target," or "I have the following issue with a supplier, and I need someone in China who can help me work through it," everything got done through my connections. Recently I was looking for people for two executive positions in my new business, and I chose to cast a broad net: I put postings on our company site and on LinkedIn. For two posi-tions I must have received a hundred résumés, among which there were some good quality candidates, but ultimately, I had to go with recommendations from my network. I've learned from hard experience that if I reach out to my network and have them endorse someone, it produces better results.

It's not just about how good you are. It's about the people you know and how you're willing to stay connected to them. Picking up the phone and cold-calling is just not the way the world works anymore. I don't know if it ever did. Anything of great value in business is going to come from someone you know and trust. Without a great network, your success will be capped. A deep, strong network is a necessity.

In business, unfortunately, the typical way to build your network is to find people who have something to offer you. For example, you come out of business school and decide that you want to work for McKinsey & Co., so the first thing you do is to contact all your B-school alums, or undergrad alums, or acquaintances from whatever club or organization you've been part of, and you try to find people who might help you. But that's a difficult way to build a network. A more effective way is to put yourself in places where you can get to know people personally and figure out how to help them *before* you ask them for something.

Networks are first and foremost built upon basic, human, interpersonal interaction—enjoying people, finding moments where you don't need them or they don't need you, moments that aren't about passing out a business card but about genuinely connecting. You need to create a bond first; otherwise, you may get a halfhearted effort or an outright refusal. But if you first look to be generous with the people you know—if you do something for them simply to be helpful, not looking for anything in return—they appreciate it and can't help but reciprocate.

The more people you know, the easier it is for you to access circles that you may not be able to reach otherwise. The person you need may be part of the network of someone you knew in school, or someone you met at an event, or someone who lived in your neighborhood. For example, I called a friend who runs a real estate investment fund in Silicon Valley. I had invested in his fund at some point, but I was really just calling him to catch up. He asked what I was working on at the moment, and I told him, "I'm on the board of this technology company, and we're trying to find a new board member. But you're a real estate guy, so you probably don't know anyone, do you?" He answered, "Let me give it a little bit of thought, and I'll call you back." A day or so later he called and said, "I know this man who lives nearby, but I don't know his technology background. Let me see what I can find out." A week or so later, my friend saw the man on the street, and they stopped and chatted. It turned out the gentleman had made $800 million in Silicon Valley, and he ran in the exact circles that we were looking to tap for our new board member. I certainly hadn't developed a relationship with the guy in the real estate fund because I thought he could find me a board member who happened to be his neighbor—but that's how it works.

You build a strong network by investing in it over a lot of years, helping people and connecting them with each other. At the beginning, it may feel like you're picking up one grain of sand at a time, and then suddenly you're picking up buckets of sand as it continues to grow. Eventually there will come a point in time—and you don't know when it will be—that they trust you and like you, and they will be helpful to you. If you continue to invest in your network, it will grow exponentially; however, if you think of your network as only useful to you, then your network will eventually become weaker. You always should be thinking, *How can I put two people together in a way that's beneficial to both?* If you can make that happen over and over again, suddenly people will want to do the same for you and for those you recommend. Then your network becomes truly wide and deep, and the amount of leverage you have explodes.

That's exactly the way Judy Robinett has built such an exceptional network. Judy is a catalyst: building relationships for her is second nature. She's never afraid to call and say, "I was talking to so-and-so, and she is working on this business," or "he's got this concept," or "she's got this problem to solve, and it sounds like something you could help with." Or she'll send me an e-mail, saying, "I met someone really interesting, and I think you have a lot in common, and you'd enjoy knowing each other." Other times when I reach out to her to say, "Hey, give me your thoughts on this issue," she always has an opinion, but usually she will add, "I know two or three people who are much deeper in this issue. I'd be glad to make an introduction."

Judy is unique for several reasons. First, I've always been impressed by how many interesting and unique things Judy has going on—she always seems to have her hands in this deal or that business or that fund, or she's off speaking somewhere in the world. Second, Judy is genuinely interested in people and has an insatiable appetite to get to know them. Connecting is her life: she's building her network all the time, so that it is always there when she needs to access it or share it with someone else. Third, Judy cares about people. The foundation of any network is how you choose to treat the people in it, and Judy is masterful in supporting those with whom she connects. To Judy, a network is simply a group of people that you trust and respect and they do the same for you, and because of that, you all treat each other very, very well.

One of the things I appreciate most about Judy is that she doesn't hold her network close but shares it freely. I sometimes find that people are guarded in sharing their network. They want to make sure they're sharing the right thing with the right people, and some relationships they hold close so as not to "overaccess" them. Not Judy: she understands that your network only expands and gets deeper the more you use it. People in Judy's network will pretty much take any call or meeting simply based on her recommendation— they have that much trust in her. The only person I've seen to match her is a man named Keith Miller, who shares all of Judy's best qualities. When I was looking to open an office for Skullcandy's Japanese operation, I sent Keith a text, telling him I was going to be in Tokyo in two weeks and asking for his recommendations of people I might talk to in order to get to know the market better. He texted back, "Give me 24 hours." Within a day he had put me in touch with the heads of Burton, Oakley, Quicksilver, Callaway Golf, MTV, and VH1. When I sat with these people, some of them said, "I know Keith well, so I'm very glad to help you." The others said, "I've never met this Keith Miller, but I'm told I absolutely have to meet you because I hear such great things about Keith." That is the power of real power connecting—and Judy has it in spades.

I define *power connecting* as figuring out how to get great leverage from your network for you and for the people you know. Not long ago I had a chance to experience the value of learning to be a power connector myself. I spent eight years running Skullcandy as it grew it from $500,000 to nearly $300 million in sales and went public, but in 2013 I resigned as CEO because I wanted to go back into the private company world, partner with a fund, and perhaps buy a business. My goal was to enjoy the process of finding a deal through people that I liked, so I spent the better part of a year just getting to know people who were recommended by folks already in my network. I'd call someone new and say, "Hey, I know so-and-so, and she speaks really highly of you. I'd love to take you to lunch sometime." "What's the purpose?" he'd ask. "The purpose is to get to know you better,"

I'd reply. For an entire year, every single day, five days a week, I had a breakfast meeting and a lunch meeting. When I was home, I'd have breakfast at Eggs in the City in Salt Lake and lunch at Sea Salt across the street. When I was traveling, I'd do the same in every city I visited. During those meals I discovered that people enjoy getting to know interesting people, but even more, they like to tell their own stories. And they appreciate it when someone makes the effort to reach out, to sit down with them and get to know them better. As I talked with each person, I tried to figure out how I could be helpful to him or her. I never said, "Hey, can you help me find a deal?"—but whenever I told people about what I was looking to do, I received countless deal and job offers. And my personal network grew richer and deeper with every connection.

A few years ago I joined the Young Presidents' Organization (YPO), which is networking on steroids. With YPO, I can call anyone, in any country, and say, "I'm with YPO, Utah Chapter; can you help me with X?" and 24 hours later, he or she will put me in front of the right person. (I also would do the same for any YPO member who called me.) It's a rare sort of network in which simply belonging gives you access to great people. But that's the kind of network you can build when you become a power connector. Power connecting is enjoyable if you think of it not as a necessity but as a lot of fun. Imagine knowing interesting people in whatever city in the world you may find yourself, and imagine being able to call them and say, "Let's have lunch." Imagine having a network of powerful connections with whom you have built strong relationships through time, and who are eager to help you with whatever you want to accomplish. Imagine being able to look at pretty much anyone in your network and know that it's okay to call them because they like you and you like them, and what you have is far more than a superficial "business" relationship. That's the kind of network that Judy shows you how to develop, step by step, person by person, circle by circle, in *How to Be a Power Connector*. The tools in this book can help you build strong, lasting connections that will ensure that you get in front of the right people, at the right time, with the right resources for your business. More important, you'll learn to enjoy the process of meeting others, getting to know them, and helping them with their goals—and seeing the enormous value that comes back to you in return.

Five years ago, if you'd asked me whether I was a power connector, I would have said no. Today I would tell you, "I'm not a power connector yet—but I'm on my way." And the lessons I learned from Judy have been part of that process. My wish for you is that *How to Be a Power Connector* will help you build the kind of rich, deep, connected network that can open doors and create greater success for everyone in it.

Jeremy Andrus
CEO, Traeger Pellet Grills, LLC
Former CEO, Skullcandy

Acknowledgments

I'm grateful to all the contributors of this book. They answered my questions, agreed to be interviewed, answered my e-mails, and were so generous with their wisdom: Adam Grant, Amy Millman, AnnMarie McIlwain, Annette McClellan, Anu Bhardwaj, Assia Haq, Audrey Beaulac, Bob Burg, Brad Thatcher, Chris Camillo, Clate Mask, David Bradford, Davis Jones, Deborah Perry-Piscone, Denise Brosseau, Dorie Clark, Douglas S. Ellenoff, Eileen Shapiro, Elisa All, Elizabeth Dell, Erin Valenti, Heidi Roizen, Iyanla Vanzant, Janet Hanson, Jason Best, Jeff Jagard, Jeffrey Walker, Jennifer Abernethy, Joseph Gonzalez, Joseph Koren, Kathy Caprino, Kay Koplovitz, Kelli Richards, Laura Leist, Lee Blaylock, Leni Chauvin, Leo Hopf, Mary Kopczynski, Michael Simmons, Natalia Oberti Noguera, Natalie Terman, Olin Wethington, Reggie Hughes, Ronna Lichtenbert, Sara Dansie Jones, Sherwood Neiss, Whitney Johnson, and Winston Perez.

A special thanks to Wendy Keller, agent extraordinaire, for believing I could do this before I knew. Thanks also to superb writer Victoria St. George of Just Write, who tested and teased my ideas to much greater depth, and to researchers Emily Sproul Cox and Trish Misiura, who helped to organize and sort the materials that added significant value to this book.

To my mother, Venna Gene: happy ninetieth birthday. And finally, to Dee, who has been telling me to write a book for 23 years.

Always remember E. M. Forster who said, "Only connect."

Introduction

FROM FRANKLIN, IDAHO, TO PARK CITY, UTAH

....

Skill is fine, and genius is splendid,
but the right contacts are more
valuable than either.

—SIR ARTHUR CONAN DOYLE

Franklin, Idaho, my mother's hometown, had a population of 300—mostly white, mostly Mormon—and for 14 years, it was my home. My dad had been in the military, but when I was 10 he retired, and we moved to Franklin. After having lived in Texas, Utah, and Wyoming, Franklin was a shock, especially when my dad marched me to the only church in town, the local LDS church. Even then I wanted to save the world, so he thought I'd grow up to be a hippie, and he figured the Mormons were a better choice.

At the beginning I wasn't happy about attending the church, but I did come to admire its focus on family, faith, and community, as well as its entrepreneurial, "pull yourself up by your own bootstraps" approach to business, education, and life. I also noticed two things. First, when Mormon missionaries went out on their two-year missions, they had to become extremely good at connecting with anyone and everyone at a moment's notice. Second, they had to learn how to take a *lot* of "no's" and just keep on going. Both of these were valuable lessons that I came to apply myself in the world of venture capital funding and building high-value relationships in business.

However, growing up I was far from a natural networker. Until I was 40 years old, I thought I was shy and felt awkward around most people. Heck, to be honest, I was terrified of people. It wasn't that I thought they were going to harm me; I just didn't think I fit in. I wasn't cute enough; I didn't go to an elite private school; I wasn't smart enough. And the idea of having to approach strangers made me extremely uncomfortable. But I also had a drive to help others in whatever way I could. You see, I firmly believe that people have gifts they need to share to make the world a better place. And I've always wanted to help people to reach their potential.

That belief and drive pointed me toward studying psychology and human behavior in college. While there I read Carnegie's *How to Win Friends and Influence People*, figuring that it might help me help others. I remember one of my college roommates telling me that she could never meet boys. I told her that she just had to say hello to random guys that she thought were cute. In six months she was married. However, I still wasn't particularly good at meeting people myself.

After college I became a social worker for the state of Idaho. I wanted to save the world; but sadly, I found out that the world really didn't want to be saved, and after three years I thought if I saw one more abused three-year-old, I'd go crazy. So I went back to school, got a master's degree in labor economics, worked in the state Office of Aging for three years, and then went to work for a Fortune 500 company. That was the turning point. I was fairly ambitious, and I wanted to move ahead in my career, and I quickly learned one of the core truths of business: *everything is about connection.*

If you want to achieve any goal, you need other people to help you do it—and your chances of success are far greater if you can help other people achieve their goals as well. I saw that there was a web, a network, of relationships that interlink individuals in every company, profession, industry, and community. When you discover those who are central to that network and you add value to them—by providing information, introductions, work, or simply helping them out in small and big ways—they will start to see you as a resource, colleague, and friend. You will become one of the people "in the know" instead of being "on the outside." This kind of high-value, strategic relationship building can help even the rankest outsider like me to become part of the "power elite."

So I worked on developing the skills that would help me feel comfortable meeting even the most important people. I started simply, introducing myself to anybody and everybody in my company. I overcame my fears and shyness by talking to people while I was standing in line in the bank or the grocery store. I made a point of introducing myself to the person sitting next to me on airplane flights. I volunteered for committees and went to group meetings, where I'd force myself to speak up. I developed networks of connections in very different arenas (a key skill for strategic relationship building), and then I'd introduce people from one arena to those in another—for example, connecting an academic with brilliant economic insights to a rising star in a hot new hedge fund. And I focused on adding value to everyone I met.

Once I started testing my theories, it took less than a year for me to develop a strong network of some of the most successful investors, fund managers, venture capitalists, and entrepreneurs in the world. This gave me the courage to leave my executive position at a Fortune 500 company and start my own business. I then became a managing director of Golden Seeds, an angel investment firm empowering women entrepreneurs. Today I am a consultant specializing in putting early-stage companies in front of angel and venture capital investors. I live in Salt Lake City, Utah, by choice. I could live in New York City, Washington, DC, Los Angeles, or the Silicon Valley—centers of influence of their respective ecosystems—but I like Salt Lake for its beautiful mountains, Park City, and the international airport. I sit on boards for companies, VCs, and accelerators; I mentor in the start-up community, work globally with crowdfunding, and speak internationally. I have taught crowdfunding strategies and business development for Draper University and Goldman Sachs's 10,000 Small Businesses program in conjunction with Babson's Olin Graduate School of Business. All of this has happened because of the 25-plus years I have spent developing my ability to do what my friends call "power connecting": finding ways to help people of all walks of life network with one another to their mutual benefit. I add value to these people consistently. That's why they're so willing to take my calls—because they know I will do what I can for them. All it takes is one e-mail or call.

One of those phone calls popped up in 2010. Stephanie Newby is the founder of Golden Seeds, and she called me about Jackie Zehner, one of the organization's members who was moving to Utah. I called Jackie and met her in Park City. We talked about her vision of women moving millions, and I shared strategy ideas and connections with her.

Three months later, Jackie called me: "Can you come up to my house for breakfast on Saturday? I have some guests in town for the Sundance Film Festival." The "guests" at breakfast included Gloria Steinem and Geena Davis (who was celebrating her fortieth birthday), as well as 30 other guests. I immediately thought of my friend "Dr. Annette," founder of Daisyclip, who had invented a permanent contraceptive device but had spent eight years trying to get it to the market. I had helped her with a funding strategy and knew she just needed the right connections.

After we all sang "Happy Birthday" to Geena Davis, I ducked into the bathroom to phone Dr. Annette and tell her, "Get your device and get over here now!" When she arrived, I introduced her to Gloria Steinem, who happened to know the number one person at the company that produces the "next day" pill and promised to talk to her contact about the device. Dr. Annette also had her picture snapped with Geena Davis, which created even greater credibility for her product. With the combination of funding, connections, and credibility, Dr. Annette was able to sell her device to a large corporation, and those of us who had invested in it received a three times return on their investment.

That's an example of the power of the right connections, and I've helped many people build the same kinds of robust strategic relationships for themselves. I've taken entrepreneurs who were shy, just as I used to be, and I've hauled them to committee meetings and prompted them to reach out to others. It has usually taken a couple of meetings, but I've watched these shy entrepreneurs blossom as they gained confidence.

Twenty-five years ago I could never have walked up to a bank president or the governor of Utah and started a conversation! But that's easy for me today, and it can be easy for you once you recognize an important truth: *every person has a gift to give and receive, and every person has problems that he or she needs help to solve.* When you engage with others by looking for their gifts and problems, and when you seek to understand and add value consistently, you will build the kind of profound relationships that will enrich both of your lives and businesses.

But for you to become a master of strategic relationships, you need to do more than just connect, care, and add value (although those elements are the most basic requirements of any relationship). You need to (1) pinpoint the relationships you will pursue and nurture; (2) reach beyond just friends, family, and profession and build a wide network of connections; (3) use a system for adding value to those contacts regularly; and (4) become the *connector between connections*—the person who can help people reach a resource they would never know about and could never reach if it weren't for you.

In this book you'll discover the inside secrets to power connecting—building high-value, strategic relationships that will help you increase your business success. You will learn to do the following:

- Think strategically about developing relationships so you can leverage your time and efforts effectively.
- Find and enter the right ecosystem that will give you access to those you need to get to know.
- Reach even the most unreachable people quickly and effectively. (The speed of response reflects the power of your connection.)
- Add value to every interaction. You have to have a compelling "value proposition" for high-value connections to pay attention to you.
- Get the contact information for almost anyone in 30 seconds or less.
- Create a 3-D connection that adds value to multiple people at the same time.
- Work key industry and community events to gain easy access to the people you want to reach.
- Seed any conversation with information about you and your interests so people will remember you without feeling that they've been "sold."
- Use one person's circle of influence to discover the lesser-known players who can add significantly to your network.
- Select suppliers, advisors, and partners that will help raise the level of connectedness and status of your business.

◆ Overcome shyness, approach strangers with confidence, and feel comfortable in any social setting.

◆ Master the four secrets of a high-value connection: be generous, caring, and thoughtful, and add value quickly.

◆ Find and use surprising and important information as a key value-add for busy movers and shakers.

◆ Create compound value by matching people to others in your network.

◆ Build a simple visual organization system to keep track of your network of high-value connections.

◆ Develop trust by doing what Stephen M. R. Covey refers to as "making deposits in others' emotional bank accounts"—favors that start at a low level to gauge interest and build trust, then progressing upward and outward.

◆ Create intrigue by discovering people's interests and offering them information or resources they might not know about.

◆ Utilize social media, e-mail, and LinkedIn effectively, so that even the hardest-to-reach influencers respond positively to your requests.

One of the most profound lessons I ever learned about relationships and connection came as a result of the Bible. When I became the CEO of a public company, we had a prominent AIDS expert from Harvard as a member of our board, and he was always telling stories about Judaism. So one day I said to him, "Maybe you can help me. When I was young, I never really understood why God let Cain live after he murdered his brother. What does Judaism say about this?"

And he answered, "God metes out the perfect judgment." Furthermore, he described that there are only two ways to make money in the world. The first way is to go off by yourself and live off the land. But the easier way is to make money from commerce and trade where people live, in cities. Cain's problem, he said, was greed.

And then it clicked: my "Cain theory of economics." The more connection, the more abundance; the more connection, the more creativity; the more things are made—the printing press, the airplane, the Internet, money, ideas, information—the better the world becomes.

Economic, personal, and professional success is about connecting the right people with the right resources in the right way, so that their value is magnified. Your success will come through your connections with other people. *Even one new connection can radically change your world.*

And, like my friend, I think that's all part of God's plan.

The Power of High-Value, Strategic Connections

Forget the MBA. Learn to network.

—JACK WELCH

I f you had to connect with a "mover and shaker" in your particular industry, how long would it take? If you needed to reach out to a powerful politician, how many phone calls would you need to place? If you needed to raise money for your business, would you know whom to contact? And would they take your calls or e-mails immediately? Do you know how to approach the movers and shakers so that they will be eager to help you with your project, business, or charitable venture?

Just like an electrical grid whose power lines are underground, invisible to the naked eye but transmitting the power that keeps our world running, there are invisible lines of connections between powerful people—connections that are unseen by most of us but that keep our global economy humming. These lines of connection have been called the "old boys' network," and their members have been called the "power elite," the "masters of the universe," or simply the "insiders." When you're a member of the group, doors open to you that are closed to everyone else. You get access to funding, invitations, information, and business deals that most people would kill for. If you're not part of the power elite, you don't just miss out on opportunities. You never even know that they exist.

In business, as in life, relationships are the *real* "power grid" that smart people use to get things done faster and more effectively. In fact, recent research stated that over 89 percent of senior executives (vice president and above) at companies with revenues of more than $100 million annually say that the strength of their personal and professional relationships has a highly significant impact on their ability to deliver business results.[1] Your contacts and connections are your most valuable assets—after all, nothing happens without them. People have the answers, deals, money, access, power, and influence you need to get what you want in this world. People write the checks for funding, and they share ideas or opportunities long before the public knows about them. People buy what your business sells—or your whole business—and they do the favors that make your path to success easier and faster.

Smart businesspeople are all too aware of the importance of strong relationships. However, the problem for businesspeople today isn't too little connection. It's too much connection. While most executives and entrepreneurs recognize that good relationships are essential to business, all too often our networking is *not* working. We're drowning in contacts, business cards, LinkedIn and Facebook friend requests, e-mails, tweets, blogs, meetings, phone calls, and text messages. We find ourselves overwhelmed by the amount of "connection" hurled at us every day.

We can't adequately evaluate the quality of the contacts we're offered; we struggle with ineffective contact management systems, trying to figure out what and whom to respond to in order to keep our lives and our businesses moving forward. A 2009 survey of CEOs and sales executives conducted by Candice Bennett and Associates, an independent market research firm, revealed that *58 percent of CEOs, COOs, and presidents agreed there was no widely accepted method for building, managing, or measuring business relationships.*[2]

All too often we fail to think strategically about the kinds of connections we need to make—who those people are, where they can be found, and how best to connect deeply with them, quickly and over the long term. The question for most businesspeople today is not "How can I be more connected?" but "How can I identify and nurture the important connections that will accelerate my success?" And equally important, "How can I connect with people in such a way that they will take my calls and help me when I need it?"

Businesspeople need a clear, workable path to find, create, and manage relationships with high-value connections that will accelerate their personal and professional success. For the past 25 years I have been studying the kind of high-value, strategic relationships that can help businesspeople gain instant access to the inner circles of influence where things get done. What I have learned has helped me go from being a shy social worker in Idaho to being a successful start-up advisor, entrepreneur, angel investor, and venture capital partner based in Salt Lake City, Utah, with six billionaires and dozens of millionaires in what's been called my "titanium digital Rolodex." I have instant access to people at international venture capital firms and billion-dollar hedge funds, as well as titans of business, academia, politics, and entertainment.

They take my calls and answer my e-mails almost immediately, even if I haven't been in touch with them for months. They invite me to conferences and dinners, host me at the most exclusive clubs in the world, and introduce me to their own high-powered connections. Not because I'm so special, goodness knows, but because I've mastered the ability to *build deep, strategic relationships that create value immediately and over time*, and to *be the conduit of information, connection, and introductions that my network could never access otherwise.* I've been called a "power connector," the "Yoda of strategic relationships," and a "relationship accelerator" because of my ability to connect with so many people at the highest levels of their respective fields. I've also helped hundreds of entrepreneurs to build their businesses by showing them how to develop high-value connections with the exact people they need.

In venture capital, your network is one of the most valuable assets you own, and your reputation within that world is critical. As someone who started as an outsider (and, frankly, as a woman in a predominantly male profession), I've *had* to develop top relationship skills in order to get access to the big deals, the latest information, and the highest levels of finance and government. I've also seen others just like me—newcomers, outsiders, people with great talents and great hearts who have so much to offer but who are struggling to gain access to the power elite. Those are the people I want to help by showing them how to get their "foot in the door" in whatever group or community they're trying to enter, and then how to build the kind of strong, smart, strategic relationships they need.

The Five Mistakes Most Networkers Make

> If we want to become successful, the traditional definition of
> networking just doesn't accomplish what is needed in
> this competitive world we live in.
> —JAY CONRAD LEVINSON AND MONROE MANN,
> *GUERRILLA NETWORKING*

Accessing the power elite starts with the recognition of one critical fact: traditional networking is no longer enough. Here are the five major mistakes I see people make when they try to network.

1. *They network in the wrong places for what they need.* Several years ago I was listening to a CD of Anthony Robbins, and he said that one of the secrets to success is massive action. I agree with him—up to a point. Every businessperson knows that action is essential, but taking the wrong kind of action (for example, handing out or collecting masses of business cards with no system for strategic follow-up) will get you nowhere. Even worse, taking action in the wrong arena is simply wasting time and energy. You can work a room until the end of time, for example, but what good will it do if you're in the *wrong room* to begin with?

As we'll discuss in Chapter 4, you've got to determine the proper *ecosystem* for your request. If you want to get a movie funded, you don't need to know venture capitalists, but you do need to know the people in the entertainment industry. If you want to start a software company, you'd better know who are the major players in Silicon Valley. And if you want to get streetlights installed in front of your business, you don't need to know the governor of the state (although it might help), but you should be able to call on your city councilperson, the mayor, or whoever is in charge of infrastructure for your community and have that person return your calls. Networking succeeds only if you're looking for help in all the *right* places.

2. *They network at the wrong level for their goals.* Instead of connecting with individuals and organizations that can provide the high-level support they need, most people spend too much time with those at their own level of knowledge and skill, or lower. If you've ever sat through an excruciating Chamber of Commerce meeting where most people are there to look for referrals, you know what I mean. And if you've achieved a certain position in your industry or community, so that everyone seeks to network with you but no one can help you gain access to the people *you* want to reach, you understand the problem. Networking at your current level may be comfortable (and in Chapter 3 we'll talk about why), but it won't get you where you want to go—and it won't help you build the strategic relationships that will accelerate your success.

3. *They have no way to assess the relative value of the connections they make.* Most of us are drowning in opportunities to connect with others—through social media, professional associations or community organizations, business leads, and so on. But we fail to "connect the dots" and figure out which connections can provide the greatest benefits. I'm not saying that you should connect with some people and ignore others; as I'll show you in Chapters 2 and 5, you never know which connections will bring you the particular resources you or someone else needs. But you have to be able to appreciate the value of every connection while determining exactly what assistance that connection brings to you and what assistance you can give in return.

4. *They have no system for optimizing their networking efforts.* Have you ever returned from a conference or business function with a fistful of business cards, only to stick them in a drawer and do nothing with them? Then you already realize the obstacles faced by most of us when we try to "network." Without a system, there *is* no strategy in your relationships. And even if opportunities come your way, you fail to seize them.

Many people think networking is simply meeting one person after another. That may create a large (and unmanageable) pool of contacts, but it will not be the kind of *strategic* networking that can help them get things done. Research clearly shows that even with all of the wonderful computer-driven tools at our disposal, human beings can build and maintain relationships with around 150 people. In Chapter 2 I'll discuss how to prioritize your connections so that you can build strong links with those who will help your business, and in the second half of this book I'll give you steps for meeting and building strong, vital relationships with anyone.

5. *They fail to network in the best way to create high-value, long-term connections.* I've seen entrepreneurs approach venture capitalists at a conference and the first words they say are these: "I need a million dollars to get my business going." Well, nobody's going to give a stranger a million dollars—that's like trying to go from point A to point Z in one step. Before people are willing to help with the big things, they must know you, like you, and trust you. And the way they will come to know, like, and trust you is through *regular, value-added contact through time.* The key isn't the number of contacts you make. It is the number of those contacts you turn into lasting relationships.

You need a plan for connecting and adding value to your network regularly. Value comes in many forms, and it is determined by the needs of the situation and the individual, but I've found that nearly everyone needs more and better information, income, key contacts, favors, and introductions. In the second part of this book, you'll learn an effective system for initiating and maintaining high-value, long-term connections with the people who matter most.

Planning Your Strategic Relationships the Way You Plan Your Business

> You have a budget and finance plan. You have a strategic plan.
> You have a plan for just about everything. But where's your
> people plan?
> —KEITH FERRAZZI

Accessing the networks you need requires an approach that is precise, intelligent, and strategic. *You need to apply the same high level of planning and strategic thinking to your relationships as you do to your business.* Strategic planning in your business gives you leverage by showing you where you must focus your efforts for maximum results. In the same way, strategic *relationship* planning can help you accelerate your professional and personal success by leveraging your efforts to connect with the specific individuals who can help you grow your business and accomplish your goals.

Let's start by defining a *strategic relationship* as *a connection between individuals that takes into account the value that each party can provide to the other—through their contacts, introductions, information, and other forms of support.* It is a "mutual assistance pact" where value is given and received by both parties. The value provided must be determined by the needs of the parties concerned. For example, a mentor provides information, guidance, and coaching to a student; the student provides energy, intelligence, and the opportunity for the mentor's influence to extend beyond himself or herself. I may provide the value of an introduction of one person in my network to another; the value I receive in return may be greater trust, more gratitude, and eventually a key introduction for me.

You have many relationships in your life—with your friends and family, your dry cleaner and babysitter, your dentist and pastor, and many others—and in these relationships, you give and receive value. However, strategic relationships are developed within the context of your professional life and business, and as such, you should bring a business approach to their development. You must assess the potential value of the people who come into your professional life not only from the perspective of "Do I want to know this person?" but also "Do I *need* to know this person?" or "Does this person *need* to know me?" You must take a strategic approach to finding and connecting with key individuals, and you must plan how you will add value to those relationships as carefully and completely as you create a plan for your business.

Some businesspeople view their relationships as assets to be hoarded and kept away from others. But I have found that the real power of strategic relationship building comes from creating *interrelationships* between the individuals you know and with their extended networks. And the more diverse and open your network of strategic relationships (what I call a *robust network*), the better. If I know people of all races, faiths, and nationalities, from the East and West Coasts and all over the world, from a diversity of professions, interests, and industries, from companies large and small, international and local, then the resources I can bring to bear to address any need I may have will be infinitely more powerful. And when you are the person who can connect the people from all of the diverse and divergent networks of which you are a part, you can provide the kind of access and promote the kinds of results that will make you a "power connector" too.

Remember, however, that the most important word in "strategic relationship" is still *relationship*. Relationships are about building connections with others who must feel you have their best interests at heart, and vice versa.

You must approach strategic relationships looking to see how you can add value *first*, creating a connection based on mutual support, respect, and liking. (In Chapter 2 we'll talk about how to avoid any potential sociopaths, leeches, and bad actors.) A strategic relationship is not like a relationship "bank," where you make deposits and withdrawals and keep a careful check on your balance to make sure things are even. That doesn't work in personal relationships, so why should it work in business? Strategic relationships must be built on a foundation of generosity, value creation, and ultimately, friendship. Your time, energy, and efforts are precious—why spend them on people whom you wouldn't want as friends?

Smart businesspeople know that, like other business assets, your strategic relationships should be accrued carefully, kept safely, used wisely, and above all, appreciated for the value they provide. In this chapter we're going to talk about the asset represented by your network of high-value, strategic relationships. You're going to discover some of the most recent academic research on social capital, and how you can turn theory to your advantage when it comes to creating your own strategic network. You see, I believe that true mastery occurs when there is both an understanding of how things work and an action plan for putting that understanding into practice. I studied economics and finance so that I could understand the basics of what makes businesses and companies successful. In the same way, I studied social networks and the way humans organize themselves so that I could figure out exactly why strategic relationships are so important—and how to develop and use effectively the business and personal value they represent.

The Business Value of Strategic Relationships

> A friendship founded on business is better than a
> business founded on friendship.
> —**JOHN D. ROCKEFELLER**

Every businessperson is familiar with the concept of capital, meaning the value, wealth, or assets held by or represented in the business. But in the last century, businesses came to recognize that the "capital" needed to make the business successful extends far beyond money or physical assets. These other forms of capital include intellectual capital (informational resources that can be used to produce profit, gain market share, create new products, or improve the business) and human capital (the skills, abilities, experience, and efforts of you and your employees). The two forms of capital that have to do with strategic relationships are *relational capital* and *social capital.*

As defined in a study by the global staffing, recruiting, and training company Adecco, relational capital is "an intangible asset that is based on developing, maintaining and nurturing high-quality relationships with any organization, individual or group that influences or impacts your business including: customers, suppliers, employees, governments, partners, other stakeholders and, sometimes, even competitors."[3] In a world in which competition is global, the advantage of separating yourself from your competition based on technology, service, or price will always be fleeting. What will set you apart over the long term is the quality of the business relationships you build.

Every businessperson knows the importance of having enough working capital available at all times to keep the business running, but it's the relational capital of your business that will do the most for your business's success. A study in 2001 of Fortune 1000 companies by Booz Allen Hamilton and the Kellogg School of Management at Northwestern University revealed that the top 25 percent of those companies focused more on relationship building than they did on sales.[4] Strong relational capital allows smaller companies to compete with bigger ones, and it allows local companies to retain and acquire new clients in the face of global competition. When companies actively seek to develop, nurture, and manage a wide network of strategic relationships, they will accrue the kind of relational capital that can lead to more referrals, customer satisfaction, and success.

Mastering strategic relationships will help you build and maintain the relational capital of your business, but it also will help you strengthen your *social* capital. Social capital is the personal aspect of relational capital. *Social capital* refers not just to the quantity but also to the *quality* and *standing* of the relationships you have both inside and outside of your business. The more connections you have, and the stronger those connections are, the more social capital you have. And the more social capital you have, the greater your opportunities.

Social capital is based on both formal and informal relationships. *Formal relationships* are those with a manager, a direct report, a business partner, your business's banker, accountant, or attorney, and so on. *Informal relationships*, on the other hand, are relationships of *choice*; they may overlap with formal relationships, but they are usually closer. You choose to develop a relationship with a colleague, a client, your manager, or your employee that extends beyond a formal relationship. As University of Chicago professor of strategy and sociology Ronald S. Burt points out in *Brokerage and Closure*, formal relationships are about authority and accountability, while informal relationships are about information, advice, cooperation, friendship, and trust.[5] Formal relationships position you in a hierarchy; informal relationships can allow you to avoid the hierarchy and get things done. Informal relationships are the real building blocks of social capital and advantage, in organizations and in life.

Social capital is also shorthand to describe the difference between an "insider" and an "outsider." Some people become insiders due to birth, social standing, education, career choice, wealth, and so on. They get the jobs, hear about the deals, are invited to the clubs or conferences or business meetings, and, in general, hang around with other insiders. As a result, they usually are paid more, are promoted faster, and receive more perks. The rest of us—those who didn't go to Harvard, didn't inherit wealth, didn't become lawyers or doctors or politicians—have to find our own ways to develop enough social capital to become insiders ourselves (or at least to gain the same advantages).

You can develop social capital in three ways. First, you can *build it yourself* by doing the things that insiders do—going to the same schools, joining the same professions, applying to the same clubs, and so on. The problem is that being an outsider trying to do all those things can be extraordinarily difficult.

Second, you can *buy it.* If you have the money and are willing to invest in the businesses, philanthropies, and interests of insiders, many doors will open to you.

Third, you can *borrow it* by developing informal relationships with those who already have the social capital you want to acquire. You are "sponsored" by an insider who then gives you entry to his or her world. Being mentored by someone is a classic method of borrowing social capital, as is volunteering to serve on committees and boards. Borrowing social capital is critical when entering different countries. For example, in places like Japan or the Middle

East, the most efficient way to do business is by being introduced by someone who is already part of the culture. (The same is true in most "cultures" whether they be businesses, professions, industries, organizations, or even families.) In my experience, the third way is the most effective because it is based on developing a strong, trusted, and robust network of connections that will help you and that you can help as well.

Just as you increase the value of a company by building its financial, physical, intellectual, and human capital, you must increase your personal and professional value as well by building relational and social capital. Building social capital requires building strong, strategic networks of colleagues and friends who will take your calls and assist you with whatever you need, and you will do the same for them. This book will teach you how to build your social capital so that it will enhance your position in your company, industry, and community; make you invaluable to the people that count; and make you a better mentor, connection, colleague, and friend for those above and below you.

The Personal Value of Strategic Relationships

> You have a good handle on your company's balance sheet,
> but do you have an accurate accounting of your personal
> net worth? If you didn't include your personal network
> in the calculations, you likely don't.
> —DAVID GELLER

Your relationships are the building blocks of your social capital. However, to maximize their value, you must think strategically about how and with what you are building your reserves of social capital, and you must understand the value that your strategic relationships represent. I believe there are 12 important benefits that a network of strategic relationships provides.

Identity

There's a saying in Spanish that translates as, "Tell me who you hang out with, and I'll tell you who you are." The people you know define you, and the "crowd" you connect with establishes your level of social status in the eyes of others. Your network is a differentiator that sets you apart from others. Your network represents you, and you represent it. If you can number high-level bankers, presidents of companies, and thought leaders among your strategic relationships, do you think people will see you in a different light than if your network focuses on the owners of struggling small businesses?

I'm not saying that you have to exclude anyone from your network. I believe that every connection (and certainly every individual) has enormous value. But we also must deal with the world as it is, and the world looks at the people you associate with as one of the key determiners of your social and professional identity.

Status

Your strategic relationships are also an indication of your status within any organization, group, or hierarchy that goes far beyond your official title or position. Proximity to the power elite can increase your status even if your title doesn't change.

Let's say you play on the company softball team, and your teammates include the vice president of your division.

One day you're walking through the halls with your manager, and you encounter the vice president. "Hi, Jim!" he says to you, giving you a high five. "Great game last week! Let's meet on Saturday, and maybe you can give me some tips on my swing."

"Sure thing, Bob," you reply.

Do you think being on a first-name basis with your manager's boss might give you an increased status? One of the reasons I suggest that people join volunteer organizations, sports teams, and cultural institutions is that it allows individuals of many different levels to meet and develop relationships that have the potential to elevate their status.

Access

Volunteer work also expands your access. I saw this in action back in Idaho. After I got my master's in labor economics, I wanted to gain greater budgeting experience before I applied for my next job. I volunteered to work on the finance committee of the board of the United Way so I could put on my résumé that I had managed a $3 million budget. Sure enough, that volunteer experience landed me the job I wanted—but it also landed me the secretary of the governor as a colleague. I was now one connection away from the governor of the state of Idaho. I knew that if I needed anything, I could call on Maria, and she would make sure the message got through. Access to the governor gave me expanded position power in my local community. Your own strategic relationships can give you access to people you should know.

Credibility

In the world of venture capital (VC) funding and multi-million-dollar deals, it's not just the deals that cause investors to open their wallets. It's also the people who *recommend* the deals that open the doors that lead to funding. A 2012 study cited in *Inc.* magazine states that the social ties between venture capitalists and entrepreneurs seeking funding are actually *more* important in the funding decisions than whether a prestigious VC firm has already committed to the deal.[6] That's a demonstration of the way relationships can give you and your requests credibility by association.

What you know is important, but *whom* you know gives you instant credibility. Being able to send an e-mail to a potential millionaire investor and say, "My client, so-and-so, your friend" (who also happens to be a millionaire) "suggested I contact you about this particular investing opportunity"—or better yet, having the client send the e-mail on your behalf—will open doors that would never be accessible otherwise.

Power

More and better connections often lead to greater power within a company, a community, or a society. You can see this play out in everything from street gangs (if you're a member of a gang, people will respect and fear you even if you do nothing) to the highest levels of business and government (why do you think lobbying firms pay high sums to employ former elected officials?). Professor Burt puts it simply: people who are better connected have more power and reap the higher rewards.

Even if this kind of power is borrowed—that is, you are powerful only because you have powerful friends—it is still a vital asset, especially when you are just starting out or you wish to enter a new community or industry. Imagine that you just graduated from college and you are seeking your first job with the local branch of "Big Bank." You have letters of reference from your college professors and from your internship in the office of the bank president. In fact, your letter of reference is from the president himself.

Do you think your application might receive more consideration? Counting powerful people among your strategic relationships will give you more clout and authority.

Information

Today there are more ways to access public information than ever before—and this means that public information provides much less of a competitive advantage to individuals and businesses. However, strategic relationships can give you access to *private* information (often before others receive it) that can be a significant competitive advantage.

Private information can take many forms—hearing about a corporate reorganization or a new job opening from the company's HR director before the official notice goes out, for example, or learning from your banker about a new competitor moving into your neighborhood, or being told quietly about a hot start-up that may be looking for investors in the near future. This kind of information is some of your most valuable currency in a strategic relationship, whether you're giving or receiving it.

And with a robust network, you never can know where the information will originate. People will call me for information, and if I don't know the answer, I will often pick 15 people from my network and send out an e-mail query. I'll get an answer back every time—but it's usually not from the person I expected. In Chapter 3 you'll learn more about building a robust network.

New Perspectives, New Skills, and Greater Creativity

Building a robust, diverse network of strategic relationships gives you access to new and different resources and viewpoints that will help you transcend your own limited perspectives and bring a more unbiased approach to your business. The members of your network can be mentors and guides to teach you new skills and show you different ways to reach your objectives. In turn, you can provide the same for others, adding value by sharing your perspectives and skills.

There is also significant research showing that strategic relationships can increase your creativity. Scientists, philosophers, artists, and creative thinkers from antiquity to the present day benefited from interacting with strong strategic networks. Freud, Picasso, Watson and Crick, and Galileo all worked or corresponded with other great minds of their times. Their different perspectives helped these geniuses solve problems in new ways and create the scientific and artistic breakthroughs that make them household names today.[7]

Leverage

In the *Oxford Dictionary*, one of the definitions of *leverage* is "to use a resource to maximum advantage." A network of strategic relationships is one of the most effective ways to gain leverage in any situation to enhance your efforts. Here's a political example. Let's say your community council is considering whether to replace the sidewalks in the part of town where your business is located. You've been asking your councilperson to do this for years, and it's finally coming up for a vote. However, budgets are tight, and your councilperson isn't encouraging, so you call the people in your network and ask them for their support.

Within days the city council has received letters, phone calls, and e-mails from prominent businesspeople and civic leaders, declaring their support of sidewalk repair. You attend the council meeting and introduce the local Catholic bishop, the president of the Chamber of Commerce, the chairs of *both* the Republican and Democratic county committees, the head of the local branch of the Small Business Association, two bank presidents, the principals of all three schools in the district, and the head of the city's PTA—all there to speak in favor of new sidewalks. *That's* using a network of strategic relationships to leverage your efforts to maximum advantage.

Your social network provides the opportunity for people to accomplish together what would be difficult or impossible for them to do individually. Every strategic connection provides more opportunities for cooperation, and like a lever, it magnifies the effectiveness of your efforts.

Multiplied Outreach

You've undoubtedly heard of the "six degrees of separation" principle, which states that most people in the world are connected by a chain of six or fewer relationships. Every strategic relationship you develop connects you to an entire web of relationships that you can call upon as needed. Indeed, you'll often find that the majority of people you need to know are in the networks of your strategic relationships.

You'll also discover that strategic relationship building provides valuable redundancy in your networks. Today I am not only one degree of separation from the president of the United States. I am 15 times one—meaning that in my network, I have 15 people who are directly connected with the president. With a diverse network of strategic relationships, if one connection doesn't lead to the person or resource you need or wish to share, you have 10 others to call upon.

Greater and Higher-Quality Opportunities

As the quality of your network rises, so does the quality of opportunities you are offered. Being connected to the CEO of your local bank, or to the president of the local United Way organization or the symphony, or to the head of the local branch of the Chamber of Commerce, for example, means that you will hear about opportunities for bigger and better deals. I know of a woman who volunteered to be part of the organizing staff at a series of professional conferences. She spent time with the conference organizer and the event planner, talking about the conference, demonstrating her own level of expertise in the field, and assisting with the running of the program. Because of her value-adding endeavors and her relationships with the organizer and event planner, she was asked to deliver a keynote speech at the next conference. Your strategic relationships can help position you to hear about and take advantage of opportunities others do not have.

Multiplied Value

Each individual possesses his or her own network of connections, which increases his or her relationship value exponentially. Conversely, your web of connections increases your value to the people you know. Imagine that you are being transferred to a new city and you have only one contact there, a former business colleague with whom you had a close relationship. You call him up to tell him that you are moving, and he says, "Great! Do you have a place to live? Let me give you the name of my real estate agent. And John's the president of the Chamber here—our next meeting is on the third Thursday of the month, and I'll introduce you. John knows everyone, so he can make sure you meet Susan, who's the best business banker in town, and Tom, the mayor. I can set you up with my accountant and attorney if you want. Lakeside Academy's the best private school we have, and my kids go there, and I'm a big donor, so if you want your kids to enroll, let me know. By the way, I'm playing golf with the president of my company on Saturday—if you're in town by then, you can join us, and we'll see about getting you a membership at the club."

That's how the world works—your network provides exponential value to others, and theirs provides exponential value to you.

Multiplied Influence and Impact

If you want to have increased influence and impact, become someone who can connect people with the individuals and resources they need but either don't know or can't access. Often people have great potential and they're just missing one thing—and when you can open a door or point someone toward a resource they need or you can help them figure out a way to accomplish a goal, your influence and impact are magnified a thousandfold.

Most people don't understand the level of influence and impact a strong network of strategic relationships can provide. I was on a plane to Israel, and I was sitting next to a scientist who has an MD/PhD from Sloan Kettering Institute, who conducts neuro-oncology research for the Huntsman Cancer Institute in Utah. She was at the top of her field but had few if any business contacts, and she was very interested in learning more about the business side of the medical industry. With one e-mail I was able to put her in touch with a colleague in Tel Aviv who specializes in medical devices and bioengineering, to their mutual benefit. I love helping people connect like that. It's almost a game, as if I'm saying, "Tell me something you would like to have happen, because I or my network can help you do it."

The bottom line is, your network is one of the most valuable assets you have—*as long as it is strategically positioned, grown, and tended so that it maintains its value.*

How Strategic Are Your Current Relationships?

> Whatever you do, whatever your level, and in whatever organization, relationships matter for your effectiveness, reputation, and success.
> —FIONA DENT AND MIKE BRENT

Now it's time to do a little relationship "inventory" and assess where you stand in terms of your strategic relationship building. Here are a few questions to answer about your current network:

1. How many of your current relationships would you consider strategic? In other words, in how many of your relationships do you focus on giving and receiving value that improves both parties' lives and businesses? What is your network's *strategic quotient* (SQ)?
2. How many people do you consistently communicate with? In how many relationships are you *actively providing value* at least once a week, month, or quarter?
3. How much do you know about the networks of the people in your network? Can you draw a picture of the spheres of influence of your strategic relationships?
4. If you needed to reach a top professional, financial, and/or political figure, how long would it take? And would that person respond to your request within 24 hours?
5. Do you have a list of high-value connections with whom you would like to develop a strategic relationship? If so, do you have a clear and written plan for reaching them?
6. Do you have a plan for managing your strategic relationships so that you can stay connected easily and frequently? If so, how is it working?

If you, like most people, feel you need to become more strategic about developing your network of high-value relationships, there are three more questions to consider:

1. *How many people do you wish to number among your strategic relationships?* Turn to Chapter 2 to discover the optimum number of people with whom you can maintain quality relationships (and stay sane).

2. *How diverse are the ecosystems in which you have strategic relationships?* There is a great temptation to build your network deep instead of broad, to develop large numbers of connections in your particular profession, industry, or community. Turn to Chapter 4 to read about the importance of a robust network that includes multiple ecosystems.

3. *How many groups are you connected to, and how many groups are connected through you to other groups?* The real power in strategic networks comes from being the "broker" who serves as the primary connection between different groups of people. In Chapter 9 you'll learn how to be the "connector's connector" by linking one group with another.

If I can create a valuable network of high-caliber, strategic relationships, anybody can do it. I was a social worker from Franklin, Idaho. I didn't know a soul with any money, power, access, or clout. But I discovered that everyone has problems that they need help solving. People with money have a problem of knowing where to put the money. People who need capital or investment are looking for the people that have the problem of knowing where to put their money. People in academia need to know about business. People in business need the validity and resources provided by the creativity and research in academia. Everyone is looking for some kind of value in what is ultimately an inefficient market, composed of a lot of other people wandering around looking for value too.

Your network is your most valuable asset because nothing happens without people. People have the answers, the deals, the money, the access, the power, and the influence, and you can access all of these resources through relationships. If you look for people whom you can help to solve their problems, and who can help you do the same, if you connect with them, add value to them first, and continue to connect and add value to them, you too can build the kind of strategic relationships that will bring you the business success you desire. And you too will become the kind of mover and shaker others seek to know.

2

Friends, Allies, and Power Connectors

....

Both B2B and B2C are dead. It is now the age of P2P
(people to people).

**—MIKE MUHNEY, COFOUNDER/COINVENTOR OF ACT! AND
INVENTOR AND COFOUNDER OF VIPORBIT SOFTWARE**

Y ou have many different types of relationships. You have friends with
whom you share common interests or history. You have important
business relationships with people whom you may never have met—
perhaps you have communicated mostly through e-mail or LinkedIn. You
may have allies, people who may be friends and colleagues and with whom
you are pursuing common goals. You have relationships with people you
meet at work, in your neighborhood or at the gym, or friends from school
you've kept up with, or those you may know through church or civic work,
or business associates from days gone by. And then there are the online "relationships" you have on LinkedIn and Facebook. (An impressive number, to
be sure: a study by the Pew Interest Group showed that in 2011 the average
American had 634 social ties in their network. Even non-Internet users had
networks of 506 people.[1]) But how strategic are those relationships? Will they
really take you where you want to go in life and in business?

Of course, every connection has the potential to enrich your life in some
way. The barista at your local Starbucks saves you time every morning because
he knows the exact way you like your coffee mocha and puts in the order as

soon as you walk in the door. The banker you've worked with for 10 years approves an increase to your credit line without question. A business associate recommends you for a seat on the board of a new company or puts you in touch with investors. Connections such as these are a part of the vast web of social capital that makes the world run. But the truth is, while you may enjoy these contacts, most relationships are not strategic. When it comes to advancing your life and business goals, you need to assess the *value* of each of your relationships.

The process of valuing your relationships is similar to that of valuing a business. You have the *core assets* of the business, which are you, your strengths, skills, and experiences. You have the *revenues* of the business, which are represented by your entire network—everyone you know and/or have done business with throughout your life. But as any businessperson will tell you, revenues are not the best indicator of the value of a business. Value is more accurately represented by *earnings*, or revenue minus expenses. (I'm simplifying here, of course.) In relationships, you can think of "earnings" as being represented by the connections where you give and receive the greatest amount of attention and, ultimately, value. While everyone in your network may turn out to be an important resource (see the following section, "The Power [and Peril] of Strong and Weak Links"), it's through your key relationships that you will receive the greatest return on your value "investment."

One method of vetting a business for investment or sale is to use a multiple of earnings as an indication of value. In the context of relationships, if earnings represent the connections where you are putting the greatest focus, "multiples of earnings" are the connections of those connections. Indeed, the value of any relationship often lies not just with the individual but also with all the connections he or she possesses. For example, when Janet Hanson, founder of 85 Broads, a global network of powerful women, spent her junior year at Mills College in Oakland, California, she was befriended by Anne Whitehead, who was a sophomore and lived in her dorm. The following year, Anne transferred to Stanford while Janet headed back to graduate from Wheaton College in Massachusetts. That fall, Anne called Janet and asked if she wanted to join Anne's family on a sailing trip in the West Indies over the Christmas holidays. On that trip she met John Whitehead, Anne's father, who was the cohead of investment banking at Goldman Sachs. "He was impressed that I was a decent bridge player and could talk about military history, specifically World War II, in which he had served," Janet recalls. "John Whitehead was the person responsible for bringing me into Goldman Sachs. After graduating from Columbia Business School at the age of 24, I joined the sales and trading desk in fixed income and never looked back."

Janet had no idea that her friendship with Anne would set her on the track of a groundbreaking financial career; nevertheless, when opportunity knocked, she jumped in with both feet. Career opportunity certainly wasn't the reason Janet became Anne's friend. But, as Scott Gerber, founder of Silicon Valley's invitation-only Young Entrepreneur Council, says, "Meaningful relationships come from meaningful connections."[2] The connections you make throughout your life will lead to other connections that just might be the key to greater success. *The value of your network multiplies by the value of the networks of the people in it.*

For example, you may volunteer for a local political campaign and get to know the candidate's chief of staff. If the candidate wins, do you think you'll have access to a very valuable network? Or perhaps you agree to be on the committee to organize a meeting for local alumni of your university. It turns out that your cochair is vice president of a thriving biotech company. When a friend's son moves to your city and is looking for a job in biotech, do you think either your cochair or one of his colleagues may be able to help? Every active connection creates a potential "value chain" that increases the "earnings" potential of your network.

Depending on whether the relationship is personal or professional, *value* can be defined in many different ways: companionship, access, support, honesty, mentoring, capital, power, and so on. And while factors such as trustworthiness, reputation, and innovation may not be represented on a balance sheet, they can dramatically affect what a company is worth. In the same way, the people in your network whom you trust, whose reputations are impeccable, and who are willing to go out of their way to help you are the ones who will provide the greatest value.

Our relationships influence our daily lives, our attitudes and beliefs, and even in a larger sense what opportunities are available to us personally and professionally. Once you understand your current relationships, you can be better positioned to maximize everything that these connections have to offer. Keep your own relationships in mind as you read this chapter.

The Power (and Peril) of Strong and Weak Links

Let your hook be always cast; in the pool where
you least expect it, there will be a fish.

—OVID

All the people in your current network can be classified as either strong or weak links. (This approach comes from sociology, and it has been applied in computer networks as well.) *Strong links* are the friends, family, and business associates you see almost every day. They are the closest members of your social network, and they usually have a lot in common with you. We all need strong links for our personal, professional, and emotional well-being; people with few or no strong links often feel socially isolated.

But there are others in your network that are defined as *weak links*: friends of friends, someone at work you might chat with on the elevator, a neighbor down the street whom you wave to as she walks her dog, a fellow alumnus of your university that you don't actually know but whom you see at a reunion, the people on Facebook or LinkedIn whom you don't actually know. Weak links are acquaintances, likely to know you by name and perhaps what you do for a living, but nothing of the details of your life. They may be distant from you because of geographical location, life circumstances, or philosophical differences.

But strangely enough, *weak links are actually the strongest and most important connections in your network.* In a study published in 1974, sociologist Mark Granovetter asked businesspeople who had recently changed jobs how they had found their new positions. You would think that the strong links in their networks would have been most useful. Instead, five out of six people had learned about the job openings through acquaintances and individuals that they knew casually through work.[3]

Granovetter describes a weak link as "a crucial bridge between two densely knit clumps of close friends."[4] Weak links are the critical connections between your network and individuals you would never have the chance to meet otherwise, but who might be exactly the people you need. In truth, the weak links in your network may be some of your greatest assets. In the funding world, often it's the friend of a friend of a friend who makes the introduction to someone who might be interested in investing in a particular company or start-up. I call such people *consequential strangers*, and in my experience, you never know which consequential stranger will lead you to your goal.

Think back to a significant turning point in your life: landing your first job, or meeting your spouse or significant other, or raising the money for your business. Chances are that a weak link connected you to that opportunity. The founder and CEO of Thought Leadership Lab, Denise Brosseau, describes a weak link that helped her at the beginning of her career:

> *When I was first getting started in business, the person who was most instrumental in my success was a woman named Leigh Marriner. Leigh was an alumna of the same college that I went to—Wellesley. Even 3,000 miles away from Wellesley's Boston-area campus, the alumnae network is very strong, and I immediately joined the local Club when I moved to the Bay Area from the East Coast. I was working in a failing start-up when Leigh posted a job opening for a marketing assistant on the Club's jobs board, and I jumped on it. Leigh hired me for my first job in the technology industry, and she became an important mentor and friend. She not only hired me again later, but I also helped her land a job when she returned to the workforce after stepping out to raise her kids.*

The strong links in your network are usually people who think the way you do and share a good deal of the same knowledge. However, some of them can be insular, and even unfavorably prejudiced toward people outside the group (some of us tend to judge people negatively who are different from us). Dealing only with people like you can also lead to conflict. According to Harvard Business School professor Noam Wasserman, who studies the dynamics of start-up companies, every social connection (friend or family member) within a founding team increases the likelihood of someone leaving that team by almost 30 percent.[5] If you rely only on the strong links in your network, you are cutting yourself off from the very people, information, and resources you might need.

Weak links, on the other hand, provide you with greater exposure to different information, situations, and perspectives from a broader cross-section of networks at every level. Weak links help you see things in new ways; they bring a richness and diversity to your world. Your weak links tie you both personally and professionally to the greater community in ways that your strong links cannot.

Weak links also exponentially increase the value of your network. With a healthy set of weak links, you don't have to be an expert at everything simply because you can gain access to the information you need fairly easily. For instance, people call me all the time to find a particular piece of information or to see if I know how to reach an individual. In response, I will e-mail a random sample of my contacts and ask them if they can help me out. Usually I will receive several replies—but the answer I seek inevitably comes from the person I think is the least likely to provide it. Weak links also can help us see a situation from a different perspective because they have a different attitude or lifestyle or have some experience in another part of the world—very valuable assets when we are looking to grow into new opportunities. Their unique knowledge and insights can pave the way for greater innovation and opportunity for you and your business. When it comes to assessing a network, the people with the greatest number of weak ties have the most significant potential to connect you with anything you need.

Your network is constantly evolving: weak links become stronger as you work with them or spend time with them; strong links become weaker as circumstances change and people move or retire or simply fade out of your life. As you look at your network, many of your connections may fall somewhere between strong and weak. However, you need both strong and weak links for your network to be healthy. For example, you will be more inclined to trust your strong links and to share more personal information and resources with them, or to go to them when you need a helping hand. You're not going to turn to a weak link first for referrals or advice—that's a little too much like a cold call. But you *can* turn to your weak links to provide the necessary introduction to one of their own strong links. Every link in your network will possess a set of connections—and your ability to link those networks is a key to your success.

Power Connectors: The Most Potent Links in Any Network

People who act as bridges between groups can become central
to the overall network and so are more likely to be rewarded
financially and otherwise.

—RONALD BURT

Among the strong and weak ties in any network, there always are a few individuals who connect many different strong and weak links, thus serving as conduits for information flowing throughout the network. In computers, such network-to-network connections are called "hubs." But there are certain individuals who don't just connect weak and strong links; they actually join different networks with each other. In *The Tipping Point*, Malcolm Gladwell refers to them as "connectors"—people whose contacts reach across many arenas and cultures, creating new chains of information, relationships, and access.

A bank president who serves on the board of his city's Meals On Wheels program persuades the members of the men's group at his church to help with deliveries two Saturdays a month. A biotech start-up wants to build a manufacturing facility overseas, and one of the scientists mentions that his father is friends with the mayor of a small town in Germany where a pharmaceutical production plant just closed. The scientist puts the company president in touch with the mayor, and the deal is done. Every new linkage of separate networks is the beginning of a new and greater entity. And in the richness of these interlinked networks lies the potential for greater growth and impact.

Such interlinked networks are an example of Metcalfe's law (another idea from computer networking). Metcalfe's law states that the potential value of a network increases exponentially with every new network connected to it. This is the fundamental principle behind the value of Facebook or LinkedIn: your position (or value) in the community is based on the number of connections you have and how those connections are intertwined with each other and with other networks. However, just as LinkedIn recognizes different levels of influence based upon the number of connections you have, I believe that there are certain people who should be called *power connectors*—because they focus consistently on connecting at an even higher level.

> *A power connector creates high-quality connections between individuals and their networks. Power connectors seek to add value by putting the best people in touch with the best resources, with the goal of creating greater success for all concerned.*

Power connectors increase the density of their networks by developing relationships between themselves and others based on generosity and mutual support. They initiate these relationships by giving value first, thus setting the stage for an ongoing chain of giving and receiving. The value can be almost anything—information, an introduction, a personal phone call, or a note. And it doesn't have to be significant, although it can turn out to be so (an introduction to a funding source, for example, or a letter of reference that lands someone a job). But usually power connectors give value without any expectation of return, knowing that the value they are providing will return to them either from this relationship or from another.

Depending on the value they add, power connectors can reach top figures in whatever arena they wish. In 2011, I had a chance to meet Rosie Rios, the treasurer of the United States, at a group called Alley to the Valley. I knew the Treasury Department was looking at crowdfunding, and as I work with several experts in that field, I offered to write Rosie a summary on the latest trends every couple of weeks. Four months later, I attended a financial conference where Rosie was on a panel. I raised my hand to ask a question, and Rosie called on me and announced, "I work with Judy." Most of the people at the conference stared at me and wondered who I was! However, I had simply done what I do with dozens of high-powered individuals as well as those I meet on airplanes and in bookstores: I was friendly, sought to add value, and then followed through on my commitments consistently. With that simple recipe, everyone can become power connectors in their own lives and businesses.

However, I have to keep coming back to the word *strategic* as it applies to creating relationships. While I always try to add value, it's just not practical to maintain strong connections with everyone I meet. Sometimes our goals just don't mesh at the moment; sometimes I can't see exactly how I can add value other than a friendly hello. And like everyone else, I have only 24 hours in a day and seven days in a week to get everything done, including maintaining connections with those in my network.

How do I sort through and keep track of my strategic connections? By understanding how the human brain works—and creating what I call *power circles.*

The 5+50+100 Power Circles

> More connections ... are less important than
> the right connections.
>
> —RICHARD KOCH AND GREG LOCKWOOD,
> SUPERCONNECT

One of the biggest problems that businesspeople tell me they face is staying in close enough contact with their networks. No matter how good your customer relationship management (CRM) system, or how assiduously you keep on top of updating your contacts on paper or in your Outlook or other software program, if you're trying to keep current with too many people, it is impossible to give them the time, energy, and attention they deserve. However, research into the way the human brain processes and organizes information can give you guidance on the optimum number of close connections to have.

One of the functions of the human brain is to identify people that are important to us and to track the member of the social groups of which we are a part. This was vital when humans roamed the ancient plains in tribes; you had to tell friend from foe very quickly in order to survive. In 1993 anthropologist Robin Dunbar wrote a paper that described a correlation between the size of the human brain and the number of people with whom a human could develop and maintain stable social relationships. According to Dunbar, the optimum group size is around 150—that's how many we can keep track of at any given time.

What if you organized your connections with that number in mind?

I believe that the *quality* of your chosen connections is more important than the *quantity*. It's very difficult to keep up with 150 people on a daily basis. Moreover, few of us truly need to communicate with 150 individuals every day in order to keep our connections with them strong. So we naturally sort our connections into smaller groups within this universe of 150, based on our relationships with them and our need for their help and support (and vice versa). Most of us have a mere handful of people we call our closest friends, family, or business associates, and we tend to see or communicate with them almost daily. Just outside of that "inner circle" are individuals whom we touch base with frequently and consider friends and associates, but they are not as near and dear as our inner circle. And then there are the people with whom we stay in touch occasionally and can call upon if needed, but we don't consider them particularly close. We naturally organize our relationships in concentric circles. What if you consciously designed your strategic relationships in that way?

I'm known as the woman with the titanium digital Rolodex, but truthfully, what I really have are three concentric "power circles" that add up to a little more than 150 people. They are categorized as follows:

Top 5. The 5 people closest to me. I connect with these people almost daily. These are the people I would trust with my life.

Key 50. The 50 important relationships that represent significant value to my life and business. I tend these connections carefully, and I am always looking for ways to add value to them.

Vital 100. The 100 people I touch base with at least once a month. Both the human touch and added value are critical to my keeping these relationships fresh.

When you organize your strategic relationships by the 5+50+100 model, it gives you a sense of control and organization that will make your life easier. The first step, however, is to evaluate your current relationships and choose who will go in which circle. I hope that you know exactly who your Top 5 are immediately. For the Key 50 and Vital 100, however, you may need to do some thinking. You want to ensure that you are selecting the best people for your power circles and eliminating anyone who may cause you harm.

The Characteristics of Great Strategic Relationships

> You have to develop a human capital network, ... people
> with whom you can be very open, who will give you
> their best advice, and you like doing the same
> thing for them.
>
> —KAY KOPLOVITZ, FOUNDER OF USA NETWORK

A few years ago I picked up a book on business strategy to read on an airplane. Usually business strategy is pretty cut-and-dried, and it's profit and loss focused; but in the middle of this book, there was this surprising sentence: "Bill Gates saved five million lives in the past three years; what have you done?" I thought, *This guy has a heart as well as a business mind!* The author, Leo Hopf, is an international business consultant who teaches at Stanford and lives in Salt Lake City, where I have a home. I contacted him, and we went to lunch, and from that lunch came the decision to write this book. But the real point I want to make is this: Leo was someone whom I knew would be a great addition to my network because of his character.

When it comes to choosing the people for your own strategic relationships, you need to select them first and foremost on the basis of who they are instead of what they have accomplished—especially if they are going to be part of your Top 5 or Key 50 circles. I asked my own Key 50 to describe what makes someone a great candidate for a strategic relationship. Their responses produced a psychological profile of the kind of person you want to include in your own network. More important, it is a description of the kind of person you should try to be.

People who create successful strategic relationships demonstrate 10 essential character traits:

1. *Authentic.* They are genuine, honest, and transparent. They are cognizant of (and willing to admit to) their strengths and weaknesses.
2. *Trustworthy.* They build relationships on mutual trust. They have a good reputation based on real results. They have integrity: their word is their bond. People must know, like, and trust you before sharing their valuable social capital.

3. *Respectful.* They are appreciative of the time and efforts of others. They treat subordinates with the same level of respect as they do supervisors.

4. *Caring.* They like to help others succeed. They're a source of mutual support and encouragement. They pay attention to the feelings of others and have good hearts.

5. *Listening.* They ask good questions, and they are eager to learn about others—what's important to them, what they're working on, what they're looking for, and what they need—so they can be of help.

6. *Engaged.* They are active participants in life. They are interesting and passionate about what they do. They are solution minded, and they have great "gut" instincts.

7. *Patient.* They recognize that relationships need to be cultivated over time. They invest time in maintaining their relationships with others.

8. *Intelligent.* They are intelligent in the help they offer. They pass along opportunities at every chance possible, and they make thoughtful, useful introductions. They're not ego driven. They don't criticize others or burn bridges in relationships.

9. *Sociable.* They are nice, likeable, and helpful. They enjoy being with people, and they are happy to connect with others from all walks of life, social strata, political persuasions, religions, and diverse backgrounds. They are sources of positive energy.

10. *Connected.* They are part of their own network of excellent strategic relationships.

Nurturing these traits will help individuals strengthen their ability to connect with others, and thus they will have stronger relationships within their networks. It will also help them to become people who develop a wide range of weak link connections, simply because they will be easy (and enjoyable) to get to know. Identify the people in your current network who already possess these characteristics: they will make excellent additions to your circles of power.

Unfortunately, not everyone in your network will live up to these standards. In fact, you may discover that you have been victimized by people like those I describe next—ones that will suck the very life out of any circle of connections.

How to Spot Leeches, Psychopaths, and Bad Actors

When people show you who they are, believe them.

—MAYA ANGELOU

Leeches are those who take but never give. They need your attention longer than it feels comfortable; they crave your praise for the smallest of efforts. They need you to help them find clients, figure out what went wrong (things are always going wrong), listen to their ailments, loan them your car keys. Their requests are endless, but if you ever ask them for a favor, they'll make it feel like an imposition. Just like a real leech, these people will latch on to you and drain both you and your connections of blood, money, access—anything they can—and then they'll be on to the next victim. Leeches come in many forms and show up in many places. They can be your subordinates or your bosses, your friends or your associates; God forbid they're family members. If you know of any leeches in your network, the only way to get rid of them is to cut them off completely.

Unlike leeches, who quickly reveal themselves as being consumed with the need to take from you, psychopaths can pour on the charm, get you to like them, and cleverly manipulate you into giving them whatever they want. Prisons are full of psychopaths, but then so are governments, entertainment businesses, and industries. (According to one study by psychologist Kevin Dutton, author of *The Wisdom of Psychopaths*, CEOs are more likely to exhibit psychopathic traits than any other profession.[6]) Psychiatrist Hervey M. Cleckley first described psychopaths in 1941 as self-centered, dishonest, irresponsible; devoid of guilt, empathy, or love; and callous and unfeeling in their interpersonal relationships.[7] They are, in a word, predators.

Psychopaths can be extremely attractive and expert at manipulating the rest of us—but they don't have any empathy or attachment to others. They rationalize their choices, but they're acting strictly out of self-interest. They are quick to blame anyone but themselves, and they have no remorse if they cause others pain. Psychopaths lie and cheat and steal and take advantage whenever they can. They are amused by your problems and not interested in helping you, only in helping themselves to whatever you have that they want. They have learned an array of methods to get what they want—by acting in certain ways and affecting certain emotions. While in business you may have to deal with psychopaths, I certainly would avoid having one as a strategic relationship.

A third group to avoid is composed of bad actors. These are people who flunk the character test. They may have great strengths and enormous expertise, but they end up breaking their commitments and cheating you of your money, time, or power. Like psychopaths, they put themselves first. They don't like to lie to your face, but they will do so if they must. They have no humility, they treat others poorly, and they can become defensive or angry if confronted. You can't trust them as far as you can throw them—but usually you don't know that until you've had the misfortune of trusting them first. If you discover you have a bad actor in your network, kick the person out immediately, and warn others of your experience with a simple "Run, don't walk" caution.

By keeping your circles free of such people, you are protecting not only yourself but the other people in your network, which should be your priority. Trust is the currency of power connecting. Your ability to screen your connections and pass along only the best to your network is the hallmark of a true power connector.

3

Make Your Network Wide, Deep, and Robust

You can be great at whatever it is that you do, but it is the breadth, depth, and quality of your relationships with others that will determine your sphere of influence and ultimate success.

—CHRIS CAMILLO, INVESTOR AND AUTHOR, *LAUGHING AT WALL STREET*

A couple of years ago I got a call from someone whom I'd never met, but who knew me through my connections in Park City, Utah. "Judy, this is Marvin Acuna. I'm going to be in town for the Sundance Film Festival next week, and I need a house where I can host a dinner for 150 movie people. Can you help?"

Of course I said, "Let me see what I can do." At the time I had no idea who Marvin was, only that he was in the film industry. A little later I was watching the movie *The Great Buck Howard* on TV, and as the credits rolled, I saw, "Marvin Acuna, Executive Producer." I e-mailed him and said, "Dude, you're famous!" He replied, "Sort of."

I got on the phone immediately with my contacts who I knew had large homes in Park City, and within a day I had found the perfect house for Marvin's party—a 17,000-square-foot property with incredible views. Marvin was very grateful, and he invited me to attend the party. A week later there I was, sitting with 150 of the top film people in the world—me, the girl from Franklin, Idaho. I was excited, but more than that, I knew this would link me with an entirely new set of networks.

I met a Hollywood event coordinator, who asked me to come to Cannes to meet Brad Pitt and other movie stars in a private event for a fundraiser for Haiti. Later she called me regarding a deal that had come up in Los Angeles that needed some venture capital (my specialty). I flew down to meet the people in her network. That single favor led to several business deals with people based in Los Angeles, and it connected me to Wendy Keller, the literary agent who represented this book.

In the last chapter I talked about the importance of having strong and weak links in your network, but it's much too easy for both your strong and weak links to represent only a very small cross-section of business, culture, politics, geography, age range, or social status. It's human nature to connect with people with whom we have the most in common. We feel comfortable with them because they share our backgrounds, circumstances, beliefs, and/ or stage of life. Social scientists tell us that we are predisposed to seek out, befriend, and like people who are similar to us (a characteristic known as *homophily*). One 2012 study at a large Kansas university and four smaller, rural colleges showed that the students at the large university, who had a bigger population of potential friends to draw from, chose people most like themselves, while those at the smaller schools, who had fewer choices, ended up with friends from more diverse backgrounds.[1]

Homophily crops up in our professional lives too. When you attend a meeting with people from different departments within your organization, do you notice that the people from the same departments usually end up talking together? Or if they mingle at all, don't the accountants talk with the accountants, the salespeople with the salespeople, and the C-level execs with each other? That kind of insularity results in closed minds, due to the biased information that group members receive and the limited interactions they have with others outside the group. Even if someone inside the group does propose a new way of thinking or suggests a different way of accomplishing a result, the ideas are almost always shot down.

Unfortunately, today more and more of us are turning to media sources and information streams that reflect our own biases and opinions. We go on LinkedIn to look for other lawyers, or entrepreneurs, or doctors, or those who share our interests. We seldom step outside our own professional silos. What's worse, every Google search and Facebook page suggestion is based on what we have searched for and been interested in before. (Did you know that the search results you receive on Google are a result of analyzing 57 different data points from your previous searches?[2]) As Eli Pariser, former executive director of MoveOn.org, describes it, we are in our own little "filter bubble" constructed for us by algorithms and websites that decide what we encounter. However, as Pariser states, "The set of things we're likely to click on ... isn't the same as the set of things we need to know."[3]

I believe the same principle is true of our connections. *The people we naturally gravitate to are not the only people we should have in our networks.* Of course, we need strong links, the people who are like us and whom we enjoy being around; in fact, they are usually the ones we choose for our Top 5 inner power circle. But a network filled with only people like you is a poor network indeed—mentally, spiritually, creatively, and often financially. In fact, too much homogeneity can actually hold you back from innovative ideas and creative connections.

In 1999 sociologist Martin Ruef surveyed 766 entrepreneurs on the connection between social networks and innovations in their businesses. He discovered that businesses with only strong social relationships among team members were less innovative due to greater pressure for conformity and lower risk taking. Businesses with team members whose relationships were more distant and whose backgrounds were more diverse tended to encourage greater diversity of ideas and more experimentation, and they had fewer concerns about conformity. *Businesses with more diverse social networks encouraged innovation at a rate almost three times greater than businesses with homogenous (only strong ties) networks.* Diversity in social networks was a key factor in producing greater innovation.[4]

Building new connections means tapping into new resources, new avenues for information and opportunity, new ways to bring people together, new potential partners and collaborators, new markets, new networks you otherwise would never be able to reach, and yes, new friends—perhaps even closer than the ones you have already. Remember that study of college students in Kansas? The students at the smaller colleges (who ended up with friends that held different attitudes, values, and behaviors) rated their friendships as closer than those of the more similar friends at the bigger university.[5] No matter how rich you believe your current network to be, it can only be better if you add more diversity, breadth, and depth.

The Three Hallmarks of a Truly Rich Network

> Early in my career, an executive in the company where I was
> working took me aside and said that I would never get
> ahead by playing an "inside game." He suggested that
> I build my network outside the corporation.
> That advice changed my life.
>
> **—AMY MILLMAN, COFOUNDER AND PRESIDENT,
> SPRINGBOARD ENTERPRISES**

To build a truly rich network, you need to step outside of your personal and professional comfort zones and incorporate greater diversity into your power circles. You must actively seek out those who are different from you—in age, experience, profession, geography, belief, politics, and culture. From them you can construct a network that is *wide, deep*, and *robust*.

I define a *wide* network as one with connections to many different industries, disciplines, locations, interests, personalities, and roles. Nowadays, of course, with social media you can connect with people all around the world. With LinkedIn, those from different industries and in different jobs can reach you with one request. However, it's up to you to look for connections in areas, professions, and interests that are *not* a natural match for you but who might expand your network into unfamiliar territories.

Diversity is key to a rich network. Indeed, a lack of diversity in your power circles can create large "blind spots" and incorrect assumptions. For instance, in the last few years members of the Millennial Generation (born between 1982 and 2004) have begun to enter the workforce in very large numbers, just as their Baby Boomer bosses are nearing retirement. These two groups see life and work very differently, and they often have large blind spots as to the needs and work styles of each other.[6] This creates problems in the workplace that might be eased simply if more Boomers and Millennials took the time to connect. Look at the people in your current power circles: Do they all look, sound, or believe the way you do? What if you were to reach out to people from different generations, other stages of life, different cultures, ethnicities, interests, or experiences?

Greater diversity in your network can decrease the number of links you need to reach other individuals, resources, or organizations. Physics professor and computer network expert Albert-László Barbarási describes it as effectively creating "crucial shortcuts" between distant "nodes." There's a famous 1967 study that demonstrates how such shortcuts can work; you may know it as the study that demonstrated the validity of the "six degrees of separation."

Harvard professor and social psychologist Stanley Milgram sent letters to a random sample of residents of Omaha, Nebraska, and Wichita, Kansas, asking them to use their personal contacts to get a postcard to either the wife of a divinity student in Cambridge, Massachusetts, or a stockbroker in Boston. If they knew the individual in question, they could mail the postcard to him or her directly. If not, they were to send the postcard to someone they knew whom they thought would be more likely to know the targeted individual. Of the 42 postcards that made it to the divinity student's wife or the stockbroker, the largest number of intermediate links was 12, and the median 5.5—but the smallest was just two![7] Coincidence? Perhaps. But I believe it's more likely that the person with just two links used shortcuts provided by a wider, more diverse network.

To be a true power connector, however, diversity isn't enough; your network also needs to be *deep* in three different ways. First, you need multiple connections in different industries, companies, interests, and so on. Say you need to reach a top official in Washington, DC; wouldn't it be better to have three or more possible contacts rather than just one? In computer network architecture, this kind of "redundancy" makes it possible for a system to function even if one or two connections go down. You want the same for your own network. Don't be one person away from power: be one by a factor of three. That way, if one link isn't available, odds are the others will work.

Second, each person you meet has an entire network of his or her own. To deepen your network, get to know the people he or she knows. Often it's not the person in your network who has what you want; instead, it's a friend or business associate who is five links away from that person. When I purchased a home in Salt Lake City eight years ago, I knew no one in the city, but within a few days I met Susan Knight, who introduced me to Mark Eaton, the Utah Jazz basketball star. Recently, out of curiosity, I decided to map out the number of connections that came from Susan and Mark. Some of those relationships are 40-deep, meaning, there are 40 links leading from Susan and Mark to some of the people in my network today. Make it a practice to actively reach out through the networks of your connections (always with the goal of adding value and acknowledging the individual who introduced you in the first place).

Third, your connections should be from different levels. I have an acquaintance who is involved in biotech, and he is always on the lookout for the next "big" device, discovery, or breakthrough. But instead of just reaching out only to the most prominent scientists in the field, he also develops relationships with their graduate student researchers. He says that often the most promising discoveries come from the students who have yet to make names for themselves. Every salesperson knows the value of developing a relationship with the "gatekeepers" for high-level executives, or getting to know the receptionist at the front desk. The more connections you have throughout all levels of the organizations and associations in your network, the better.

However, a deep network must contain links to people *above* you as well as below and at the same level as you. It's very comfortable to build a network of gatekeepers, those on the way up, and those whom you consider your peers. It's a lot harder to reach out to individuals whom we admire or whom we perceive as having more power, access, or money than we have.

I can't tell you how many times someone has come to me for advice or help, and I'll say, "E-mail so-and-so, she's the CEO of the company, here's her direct e-mail," only to discover later that the contact never occurred. When I ask why, the response is usually something like, "Oh, I didn't want to bother her," or "Why should I? She won't get back to me anyway." It may be comfortable to swim with the fish at your level, but you can lose a lot of time and, more important, credibility with the movers and shakers at higher levels if you are perceived as only a peer of their subordinates.

In later chapters I'll talk about ways to reach pretty much anyone (hint: it's about adding value; plus, most people at high levels are actually very open to the right approach), but you must make connecting "upward" a priority. Think of your network in three dimensions rather than two, and make sure you reach up as well as down and sideways. As long as you're polite and respectful, what do you have to lose by reaching up and out?

The last feature of a power connector's network is robustness. To me, a *robust* network is (1) competent, (2) responsive, (3) interconnected, and (4) similar in values while diverse in everything else. Power connectors are all too aware of the limits on their time, energy, and focus; that's why they are very selective about the people they bring into their 5+50+100 power circles. Therefore, even if someone is just getting started in his or her career or profession, I believe that he or she should demonstrate high levels of competence to be considered for referrals. Every recommendation I give reflects upon me, so I am very careful about the people I refer to others and the introductions I give. That's why I seek out the best of the best to enhance the robustness of my network. To me, competence is an entry-level requirement.

One of the clearest indications of the robustness of your network is its responsiveness. Do people return your calls or e-mails promptly? Do they listen to what you say? Are they helpful? When you introduce one of your connections to someone new, will your connection take the time to reach out based simply on your recommendation? I am proud of the fact that in my power circles, the people I reach out to will listen, see if they can help, and usually do what they can for someone within 24 hours. (They often laugh and say, "If Judy thinks I should know you, I should.") A responsive network is a strong indication of the amount of value you have provided to its members over the years, and your status in their eyes. And naturally, you need to be just as responsive when someone in your network makes a request of you.

A robust network is rich not just in connections but also in *interconnections*—that is, the interrelationships between its members. Power connectors work as hard to link members of their networks with one another as they do to develop new connections. They know that the real "magic" of a network arises when people—black, brown; Christian, Jewish, Muslim, Buddhist; East Coast, West Coast; Europe, Asia; North America, South America, Central America; Republican, Democrat, independent; artist, entrepreneur, corporate executive—meet and form new relationships.

The last, and most important, quality of a robust network is a shared set of values. I believe in diversity in all things *except* in the fundamental principles of authenticity, honesty, fair play, caring, and a focus on giving to others. Those values are the price of admission to my network. Those shared values mean that I can have complete confidence in the members of my network to keep their commitments, help others, tell the truth, and seek to create the best outcomes for all concerned in any interaction. Maybe insisting on these core values makes me old-fashioned, I don't know; but I *do* know that those values help ensure that my network remains high quality, high value, and robust, and something of which I am proud to be a member.

What to Look for in Wide, Deep, and Robust Connections

> Sometimes you don't have to travel the world to make a good connection. You just need to know where to look—and it might be in unexpected places.
> —DEVIN THORPE, AUTHOR AND
> *FORBES* BLOGGER

When you reach outside your comfort zone of connections and seek to expand your network, it's helpful to have some specific criteria for the new additions. Here are a few suggestions about the kinds of people to look for—and a few unexpected places to find them.

Get to Know People Who Don't Agree with You

The world can be pretty small when you're surrounded by people who echo your opinions. You can even be fooled into believing that everyone thinks the way you do. However, listening to and trying to understand people with different opinions are essential skills for developing not just a more robust network but also a more robust view of the world. Remember, you don't have to agree with their views; but if you can get past any disagreements, you may be surprised to discover how much you have in common.

You may be a fundamentalist Christian working side by side with a liberal agnostic, and you discover that both of you are passionately committed to being a Big Brother or Big Sister. Or perhaps you're an East Coast sophisticate sitting next to a Texas cowboy at a football game, both of you cheering for the home team. Or you see a recent immigrant walking side by side with a law-and-order advocate to raise money for cancer research. As long as you have some basic values in common, people who don't think exactly as you do can bring a raft of different experiences and views that will broaden your perspective and enrich your network.

Look for Geographical Diversity

Say that you want to buy a beach property rental business, but most of your connections are in the Midwest. Or a friend calls you for advice about investing in a factory in India, but you have no contacts anywhere in South Asia. Greater geographical diversity in your network will bring a wider variety of ideas and interesting people into your network and make the world feel smaller. It will also help you access the right resources and the right people in the right areas of the world. And today, with sites like LinkedIn and services like Skype, developing connections anywhere in the world is easy.

Look for Personal Diversity

Find people with wide-ranging interests and passions—there's nothing more boring than a bunch of people who do nothing but talk business because that's all they have in their lives. Don't get me wrong, I love business and find it infinitely fascinating, but I don't want that to be the only aspect of my life that I'm passionate about. Nor do I want to be around others who believe that if we have business in common, that's enough. Human beings need humanity: by that I mean we need to be with people who have passions, interests, and experiences different from our own.

One of the best ways to build strong strategic relationships with others is to ask them about the parts of their lives that have nothing to do with work. Ask about their families; ask about their hobbies, vacations, and causes. First, you may find more points of commonality upon which to build the relationship, and you also may discover an entirely new network of people who share your mutual passion. Second, their passion just might trigger something new in you, and the next time they go scuba diving, or plant a garden, or stump for a local political candidate, you may find yourself going along and enjoying yourself immensely, enriching your life as well.

Look for Professional Diversity

Step outside of your business and look to community, academia, and associations for new relationships. In 1997 a group of women who worked at Goldman Sachs founded 85 Broads, a global women's networking association with a mission of "generating exceptional professional and social value for its members." Today, with members who work for nonprofits and for-profit companies in more than 130 countries, and campus clubs that enroll both graduate and undergraduate students, 85 Broads connects an exceptionally diverse population of women worldwide. According to the organization's website, "The women in 85 Broads are entrepreneurs, investment bankers, consultants, filmmakers, lawyers, educators, athletes, venture capitalists, portfolio managers, political leaders, philanthropists, doctors, engineers, artists, scientists, full-time parents, and students."[8]

Groups like 85 Broads help power connectors to increase the amount of professional diversity in their networks. Look around: What are the fields that complement your business and/or interests? Where else can you go for valuable contacts who can bring you new information and resources, and for whom you can do the same? For example, professors in your field at a local university can give you access to new academic research. Professionals in different industries may provide alternative approaches to problems you may be encountering on the job. Reaching out through networks on LinkedIn and Twitter can keep you up-to-date on the latest trends. Find the places in which interesting people are already congregating, and put yourself into the milieu. Your resources may enrich these new arenas while you gain valuable "out of network" connections.

Look for Other Connectors and Players in Their Fields

In his book *Linchpin: Are You Indispensable?*, marketing expert Seth Godin described linchpins as "the essential building blocks of great organizations." Every network also has a linchpin, someone without whom the network would not function as effectively. This individual isn't necessarily the one with the greatest social status or organizational power, but he or she inevitably is the most informed and/or helpful. The television show *Suits* focuses on the interoffice affairs, fights, and intrigues at a top New York law firm. Most of the characters are high-powered attorneys—but the linchpin in the office is a legal secretary, Donna. Donna talks to everyone, and everyone talks to Donna. As a result, she knows everything, usually before anyone else, and she wields great power simply due to her connections. Connectors and people influential in other fields can become valuable allies. If you can identify and link with linchpins like Donna, you will find it easy to access anyone in his or her networks.

Some linchpins also have capabilities and expertise that make them *players* in their respective fields. Sometimes referred to as "opinion leaders" or "influencers," players are recognized both for their ability to get things done and their connections to others who can do the same. Players and linchpins benefit from a principle described in computer network theory as "preferential attachment." This means simply that, in the same way "the rich get richer" and the most popular results are listed first on a Google search, the people with a lot of connections attract even more connections to themselves. Put simply, people wish to network with those who are highly networked already. Adding linchpins and players to your network will immediately multiply your reach and influence significantly. As long as these individuals share your values, they will be some of the most important additions you can make to your circle of connections.

While linchpins and players wield great power in their respective networks, the real key to building strong strategic relationships is to connect disparate networks with one another, and that's what power connectors do. They allow resources, ideas, people, places, and organizations to connect more easily and directly. Like hub airports such as Chicago or Dallas, power connectors allow smaller, less connected individuals to link with others who might never meet otherwise. They provide trustworthy and informative sources of new ideas, opposing points of view, and different approaches to old problems. They stimulate collaboration between groups and individuals. And if their network is wide, deep, and robust, they can introduce others to new ways of thinking, acting, and above all, connecting.

The Right Ecosystems Will Determine Your Success

....

*If you want to go fast, go alone. If you want
to go far, go with others.*

—AFRICAN PROVERB

For the past 20 years I've helped all kinds of entrepreneurs and companies across the world, but remember, I started out in Idaho—not exactly a crossroads of international finance—as a social worker. I quickly learned, however, that in every community, business, or organization, there are centers of activity and influence, and in order to get much of anything done, you need to (1) understand where they are, and then (2) access them strategically.

In Idaho, one such center was Boise, the state capital. I was working as a planner for the state Office of Aging in Boise, but I had bigger ambitions. I also realized that if I wanted to get into private enterprise, I needed to add to my experience outside of government. So I volunteered to serve on the finance committee of the Boise chapter of United Way. I figured it was a great way to learn to manage large budgets (and it was—United Way's budget that year was $3 million, a staggering number to me at the time). That particular skill set, and the line on my résumé, landed me my next position as a manager in a Fortune 300 company. But my volunteer work also put me in the room with a number of important people in the local community. I connected as a peer with business CEOs and C-level executives, the heads of colleges and universities, and players from other nonprofit and state agencies. I also got to know the secretary of the governor of Idaho. Most important, through that experience I learned about the power of *ecosystems*.

Webster's Dictionary defines an *ecosystem* as "the complex of a community of organisms and its environment functioning as an ecological unit." In business, I believe an ecosystem is *a web of professional and personal connections who are linked by common interests and who share knowledge and access unavailable to outsiders.* Every potential source of money, assistance, or expertise has its own ecosystem. Your family is an ecosystem. Your business is an ecosystem. Politics at every level is an ecosystem. The media make up an ecosystem. Money is *definitely* an ecosystem. In fact, the whole world is composed of ecosystems that channel power and influence from one member to another. The ecosystems in which you participate define you, both to the people in the system and also the people outside it. When you become part of an ecosystem, you have four vital advantages: knowledge, connections, resources, and opportunities.

Knowledge. While you may be extremely well informed about your own field or industry, tapping into experts in other ecosystems (and even in your own) can provide you with fresh knowledge not found in books or through any other "open" channel. For example, say you're an executive with an Internet company, and you have cultivated connections in the state political ecosystem. They can keep you abreast of any pending legislation relating to Internet sales taxation, thus allowing you to make your voice heard in the discussion before it comes to a vote. In his book *Give and Take*, Wharton professor Adam Grant tells the story of the man *Fortune* magazine called its "best networker," Adam Rifkin, who is a legend in the high-tech community of Silicon Valley. Through his organization 106 Miles, Rifkin freely shares with members his knowledge about industry trends, job openings, possible sources of funding, and so on.[1]

Connections. People in ecosystems are more likely to help give you access to others in the same system. A friend of a friend has a son who plays Pop Warner football with the son of the general manager of the local professional football team. On "Meet the Players" day, the GM arranged for the boy *and* his parents to have photos taken with the team's top stars. Another acquaintance worked with a real estate agent to sell her house in one community in Southern California before moving to another city. The agent then made a call to connect her to an associate in the new city and gave the woman referrals for local appraisers and inspectors.

Resources. You already know that your connections will get you access to resources you could never reach on your own. But when you're in the right ecosystem for your goals, those resources are often targeted and of extremely high quality. I see this all the time with venture capital deals. The entrepreneurs who have taken the time to develop connections in the VC and financial world usually get introductions to the specific firms that are best suited to their start-up proposals. Entrepreneurs who approach the financial ecosystem only when they need money immediately have less of a chance of getting the right match.

Opportunities. Every ecosystem provides a wide range of opportunities to its members that outsiders never hear about until much too late. As someone who sits on VC and accelerator advisory boards, I see the power of these "hidden" opportunities all the time. One gentleman I know started a company in Utah, with the idea of selling the business within a few years. So he anticipated which other companies in the same field (ecosystem) might be likely to acquire his business. He asked three individuals from those companies to sit on his advisory board. When the owner announced that he was open to a sale, the three companies ended up in a bidding war. The owner sold his business for $45 million after just three years of operations—unheard of for a drug development company.

Anything you want to achieve—start a business, write a book, raise money, find the best preschool for your child, and so on—has an ecosystem, and you have to know how it works. Unfortunately, few people understand ecosystems, or even know they exist. They work hard trying to get ahead, but their efforts are misdirected and thus often wasted. It's as if they've read the books on how to work a room, but they have no idea *they're in the wrong room!* To be successful in anything, you must understand the ecosystem that is most relevant to your particular goal and then build rich connections with the people in that system.

Here are some key basics about finding and joining ecosystems.

Ecosystems may be location specific. If you want to access the political ecosystem, you'd better plan on a trip to Washington, DC, your state capital, or your local city hall, depending on the level you wish to reach. If you want to be involved with entertainment and media, in the United States the decisions are made in New York and Los Angeles. You've got to know where to find the influencers in your particular industry and field. I am based out of Utah, but I spend a lot of time traveling to New York City and Silicon Valley to stay current with the venture capital, financial, and technology ecosystems. Certainly, you can connect with ecosystem members online through services like LinkedIn and by attending conferences and meetings, but you'd better be willing to go to the centers of power for the ecosystems you wish to reach.

Depending on your business and networking needs, you also need to develop different strategies for local, national, and international ecosystems. For example, West Coast and East Coast funding ecosystems are very different; the same approach will not work for both. And if you try to use U.S. strategies in ecosystems overseas, you could be in trouble. You must get to know the specific ways each ecosystem is different.

You must develop connections with more than one person in the ecosystem. As I said in Chapter 3, your network needs to be deep, meaning that you have multiple connections in any given organization—and that holds true in ecosystems as well. Luckily, there are thousands of people in each ecosystem who might be potential connections. Do your research in advance so you can approach the specific people you need.

You must know how the ecosystem works. In the world of venture capital, you can't just walk into a VC firm and say, "I have a great idea, wanna invest?" Nor can you walk up to a movie executive, hand him or her a script, and say, "Make my movie!" You have to find out how the ecosystem works before you attempt to join it. While some of the information you need is available through books, I once heard someone say that you can learn more by talking to someone for an hour than by reading books for a month. The best way to figure out the workings of an ecosystem is to approach individuals who are part of it, provide them with value, and then ask them to teach you what you need to know.

You must actively seek to develop trustworthy relationships with the people in the ecosystem by adding value and keeping your word. You must prove yourself to be trustworthy and likable to the members of any group. You do this by adding value consistently and keeping your commitments when you make them.

While the ecosystems you need are as varied as your goals, I believe that certain ecosystems are vital for everyone's success. However, if you are in business, you had better gain access to the five critical ecosystems described next. By the way, you also have your own ecosystem: your power circles, or your network. You must be very careful who you let into this ecosystem, as it's the most important asset that you have. And make sure it includes people from many different ecosystems, and that they all reflect your values.

Eight Key Ecosystems Essential for Your Success

> Every person is defined by the communities she belongs to.
> —ORSON SCOTT CARD

I believe that, once our basic needs are covered, we tend to focus on three fundamental areas or ecosystems: *family and friends, passions and interests*, and *career or profession*. In business, the ecosystems of *government and politics, finance, media, industry*, and *community* are also essential. Whenever I moved to a new city, I would seek to make friends with the editor of the paper, county commissioners, investors, and local businesspeople. That way I could source any knowledge, influence, money, and connections that I might need. That's the power of connections in a wide range of ecosystems.

Here are the eight key ecosystems that, depending on your goals, should be represented in your network.

Family and Friends

While other ecosystems may lead us to greater success, this is the ecosystem I love. I believe that friends and family give us the greatest sense of fulfillment. If you have strong relationships within a healthy ecosystem of friends and family, don't you find that it makes things better even if business is tough? And conversely, if things are great in business but you're having trouble at home, or worse, you have few or no close connections, isn't there a hollow feeling at the center of your success? Connections with friends and family enrich our lives more than any other, so it's important for our ultimate fulfillment that we spend time and effort here.

That said, friends and family might provide valuable connections both personally and professionally. Perhaps your brother-in-law may turn you on to a new client or a job, or you might find a great attorney through the parents of one of your children's friends. Or you may be able to help out a friend who needs a hand. One man I know, Mark, received a call from a college roommate he hadn't seen in 30 years. The roommate's son was moving from New York to the city where Mark lived. Would Mark be willing to check out an apartment that the young man had seen online? Mark not only went to look at the apartment but he also took pictures and drew out the floor plan. The young man rented the apartment and is now happily living in a local beach community while attending graduate school. There may be little professional benefit when you add value to your friends and family ecosystem, but the emotional rewards are usually higher—and well worth the effort.

Passions and Interests

This ecosystem is flush with possibilities for information you don't possess and connections you would not make any other way. I have a dear friend, an Israeli, who is an investor focusing on genetic research, and I have introduced her to several people in my power circles. Not too long ago she mentioned that she had approached a billionaire couple with interests in both Israel and the United States and asked them if they would be interested in any of her projects, but they declined. "You're going about this the wrong way," I told her. "Wealthy people follow their passions—be it the arts, social causes, politics, whatever. You need to find out what this couple is passionate about, and if you can share their passion, you need to enter that ecosystem by adding value with your time, money, or connections."

Our passions enrich our lives in ways our professions cannot. We become more interesting and unique people when we're talking about our favorite sport or sports team, or the time we climbed Kilimanjaro, or our collection of Grateful Dead memorabilia, Harley-Davidson motorcycles, or first editions of Dickens's novels. And people are passionate about everything under the sun. "Do you like Scrabble? Table tennis? Wine tasting? Cooking? Tea? Bill Murray?" asks the founder of Concept Modeling, Winston Perez. Attending and/or creating events around the things that interest you personally are better ways to network than going to so-called networking events." When you connect with someone over a passion, it's a far more natural and authentic relationship.

Career or Profession

Whether you're a "solopreneur" working for yourself, or you hold a position in a small or large company, or you're the owner of a business of any size, that career or profession has an extensive ecosystem. It includes your organization plus all of the professional connections that are linked to it: suppliers, buyers, CEOs from competing companies, financial advisors, consultants, IT support teams, and service providers of all kinds.

How closely are you connected to others within your professional ecosystem? Are there individuals in this ecosystem who could open doors for you, or whom you could affiliate with and benefit from the relationships they have already developed? Do you actively seek to develop trustworthy relationships with the people in your professional ecosystem by adding value and keeping your word? It's all too easy for many of us to silo ourselves in our jobs or our businesses. Truly successful people know that greater success and advancement come from greater access and influence within their professional lives.

Government and Politics

Developing connections in local (and perhaps even state and national) government will make your life easier and help gain you greater knowledge, connections, access to resources, and opportunities. There are many different paths into this ecosystem. Make sure that you know your local government representatives and that they know you. Volunteer for committees and commissions. Invite your local representative to industry functions. Express your opinions about local issues that matter to you. Show that you are interested in the efficient running of government in your community.

You can do any and all of this in a nonpolitical way, if you desire. I started my career as a state employee, and so I could not express a political opinion. But by offering my own knowledge, connections, and resources to the elected officials of the state, I was able to enter and eventually even have a small amount of influence within the government ecosystem in Idaho. Since then I have made it a point to respond to requests from many elected officials to serve on commissions or to help with their efforts to improve the city and state where I reside. However, I will say that getting involved in the *political* side of government is a much faster path to the heart of this ecosystem. Power, money, and politics are closely intertwined. Every politician is interested in donors, supporters, campaign workers, and endorsements from the business community—and if you can provide any of the above, politicians will take your call.

Finance

This is the ecosystem in which I work. Unfortunately, that means I see the mistakes that people make when seeking to gain access and resources here. Individuals call me or send me e-mails every week wanting to find money, and they think if they just keep knocking on doors, eventually one will open. But they don't understand how the venture capital community works. You must build relationships with investors early, and you must remember the basic premise of all power connecting: *add value first.*

In business, the people you know, the people who refer you, and the people you've done business with consistently will often open more doors than your pitch, idea, story, or business plan. Even if you're just getting your business off the ground, get to know your banker. Add value by being a good customer, one who pays bills on time. Care for the bank's money as if it were your own. And remember that a banker is a human being, someone you can connect with by asking about family, sharing interests, contributing to his or her charities, and so on. While a personal relationship will not trump fiduciary responsibility, it might add to the warmth of the recommendation when your application goes before the bank's lending committee or when an investor calls to check out the health of your company.

Media

Every businessperson needs to be aware of, if not connected to, the media ecosystem for their own locality at least. Coverage from local news outlets can let other people know about your grand opening, your community service work, your plans to expand (and your need for financing), and your awards, milestones, and successes.

Media coverage is also a great way to get on the radar of movers and shakers in other ecosystems (community and industry, for example). Most media outlets are constantly on the lookout for good stories and good sources; if you can provide both, it's relatively easy to develop relationships within this ecosystem.

Your Industry

This is an area where you can develop some of your richest and most valuable connections. I always suggest to people that they draw a map of the ecosystem of their industry so they can see how many possible avenues there are to create relationships. In the biotech industry ecosystem, for example, you have "Big Pharma" companies, VCs who fund start-ups in life sciences, doctors, hospitals, pharmacies, attorneys and accountants who serve this field, professional organizations like the Biotech Industry Association, conferences (the biggest being BIO), scientific journals, writers who focus on biotech for different media outlets, and universities with professors and researchers specializing in life sciences. And all of these people and organizations can be found at the local, national, and international levels. I suggest to people that they map their industry ecosystem as concentric circles, starting locally and expanding out from there, and then look for ways they can connect strategically with people in the different circles.

One of the easiest ways to find groups in your ecosystem is by using the Internet. Follow thought leaders, bloggers, and writers in your industry on Twitter. Join communities and discussion groups on LinkedIn. Keep abreast of news and the latest developments by joining professional organizations and reading the news releases and journals they put out. Keep up with news about your industry in general, as sharing information is a powerful way to build and maintain connections with others. However, the biggest key to success in your industry ecosystem is to become an active participant in it. Join industry-related groups, and volunteer for leadership roles. Attend conferences. (In Chapter 10 you'll learn strategies for maximizing connections at conferences, conventions, and meetings.) Reach out to others in your industry to offer assistance and to understand their perspectives. As my friend Leo Hopf has pointed out, all of these activities in your industry ecosystem are "not as much about networking or increasing your business but about getting yourself inserted into the power structure of your particular field or profession."

An area that is often overlooked in the industry ecosystem is the academic and research side. I believe in many industries there is too little back-and-forth between academic experts and those of us on the front lines of business. Certainly, we are seeing more conversation and collaboration nowadays, but I believe there is room for improvement. If we take the time to reach out, both parties will find the connections that can bear significant fruit.

Most of us encounter academic experts through the books they publish. I have made several significant connections simply by reaching out to authors from academic settings. Eileen Shapiro (who is a past consultant at the global management services firm McKinsey & Company) coauthored *Make Your Own Luck: 12 Practical Steps to Taking Smarter Risks in Business,* with the Sarofim-Rock Professor at Harvard Business School, Howard H. Stevenson. I was so impressed with the book that I called Eileen's company, the Hillcrest Group, to request some information on her. To my surprise, I got Eileen on the phone—and she was thrilled to talk about her book. Because of that contact, Eileen and I have worked with many start-ups together. She also introduced me to Howard Stevenson. Even if you never attended Harvard or Stanford or another prestigious university, you can access the power of their ecosystems simply by reaching out to the academics that teach and do research there.

Community

This ecosystem is one of the most important in terms of your local standing and ability to add value close to home. "Business relationships are important for strong communities," says former president and board chair of the General Mills Foundation Dr. Reatha Clark King. "The business, nonprofit, government, and faith sectors of society all have uniquely valuable functions and contribute to a community's success and stability." Sara Dansie Jones, an intellectual property attorney and founder of IFINIDI (a technology consulting and product development firm) describes the benefits she received from contributing to her community:

> *Rick Nydegger was one of my professors in law school, and then he sponsored me being hired at his firm. But he supported me in activities beyond just practicing law, which, over a 10-year span, included running firm recruiting and events, directing the IP moot court competition for both of Utah's law schools, serving on the Brigham Young University (BYU) law school alumni executive board, being an adjunct professor at BYU law school, and launching the Women Tech Council. I remember early on Rick told me that giving back to our larger community would be one of the most rewarding parts of my law career, and he was right. It also started my journey of developing a very rich professional network.*

Under "community" I also include charitable networks, social and religious organizations, schools, and arts and sports groups as well. Becoming an active participant in your community ecosystem will give you access to relationships and people you would never have otherwise. There's a great story about Bill Gates's mother, Mary, serving on the board of United Way with a top IBM executive. Because of their connection, she was able to talk with this gentleman about the way IBM was ignoring newer, smaller, more innovative companies in the computer industry and going with larger, traditional firms instead. Not long after, IBM began taking proposals from smaller companies, one of which was Microsoft.[2] Bill Gates's rival, Steve Jobs, also wrote a blog that said, donate to the charity of the person you want to meet, or volunteer for his or her favorite cause.

Notice that the word "volunteer" crops up a lot when it comes to adding value to different community ecosystems. A friend who is a networking expert and very savvy about volunteering suggests, "Select one group and become active in it. Go to meetings regularly, and take a position on the board of directors. By doing this, you create visibility within the organization and you have the opportunity to show people what a good leader you are. When you deliver first-class work as a volunteer, people will assume you deliver the same high-quality work in your professional life."

Finding and Contributing to the Important Players in Each System

> Surround yourself with people who are going to lift you higher.
> —OPRAH WINFREY

Before you attempt to enter an ecosystem, be sure of three things. First, who are the people you wish to meet? Do your research and identify the individuals who could be rainmakers, door openers, power connectors, or mentors for you and your business.

Second, determine what you have to offer them rather than focusing on what you need. What are you willing to invest in these potential relationships? What knowledge, connections, resources (including time, money, support, and emotional buy-in), or opportunities can you share before you ask for anything from them? You must be prepared to make a substantial investment up front in order to reap the benefits of any relationships in a new ecosystem.

Third, make sure you are a good fit for the ecosystem before you try to enter it. If you are going to network up, you need to dress and act in ways that are appropriate to the level you aspire to rather than the level you currently inhabit (if it is different). I once read that Charles Lindbergh was an expert at connecting with powerful people, but he had to be taught to "dress for success" so he would fit in. The higher you go, the more you need to have your "rough edges" knocked off. (Of course, there are iconoclasts who break this rule, but if you look closely, I think you'll see that such individuals bring so much value with them that others are willing to make allowances.) It's much easier to enter an ecosystem—in particular, one inhabited by movers and shakers—when it feels to its members like you belong there.

Once you've identified the people you wish to reach, decided the level of value you are willing to add, and done what you can to become a good fit for the ecosystem, you need to initiate contact. I'm sure you've heard the expression "Birds of a feather flock together." The same is true in each ecosystem: those with power tend to go to the same meetings, belong to the same clubs, and be invited to the same events. For example, there are clubs of every kind in every major city in the world. At many conferences and industry meetings, there are executive memberships, VIP tickets, private receptions, and so on. You must be willing to invest up front in joining these group occasions. You may need an invitation, or you may just need to pay for access. Regardless, when you arrive, keep your focus on adding value with appropriate knowledge, connections, resources, and opportunities.

Finally, within each ecosystem you must do what you can to add value, and not just upwards but sideways and downwards as well. With each value-add to any ecosystem member, you are building social capital based on your genuine interest in helping others to accomplish their goals. Better yet, figure out how their goals and your goals coincide. Remember the definition of an ecosystem: *a web of professional and personal connections, linked by common interests, sharing knowledge and access unavailable to outsiders.* When you can add value to the common interests, common goals, common purposes, and common efforts of an ecosystem, you will quickly become an integral part of it—and thus become a mover and shaker yourself.

5

The Power Connector Mindset

....

As an entrepreneur I find people fascinating: they have experiences and insight that I don't have.... You have to genuinely like people to make this work.

—JENNIFER ABERNETHY, AUTHOR AND SOCIAL MEDIA MARKETING EXPERT

Once you've identified the right ecosystems, it's time to connect—and how you go about making those connections is of critical importance. You'd think this would be easy because on the most basic level, humans are born to connect with one another. Babies notice facial expressions from their earliest days of life as they begin to recognize the emotion in their mothers' faces. When we learn to talk, we seek not only to name things but also to tell others about them, engaging those around us in conversation about mutual experiences. But somehow when we step into the world of business, the joy of engagement is often lost in our efforts to give away one more business card or add one more name to our list of contacts. Or worse: we ignore others in the room and spend our time seeking out and sucking up to the few powerful individuals who we think can do us the most good.

I believe that the mindset most people have about developing business relationships is what gives networking its bad reputation. People accumulate contacts but reach out only when they need something—a favor, a sale, or an introduction. They convert what should be a business relationship or a connection into a business *transaction*, of the "I need you now" but "Who are you again?" later kind. You can't wait until you need relationships to develop them. You need to build your relationships early, and you need to base them on the same criteria as every other relationship: respect, mutual values, and a desire to benefit all parties. These fundamentals are the foundation of the *power connector mindset*. Once you adopt the power connector mindset for your own, the people you meet will remember you and consider you a great addition to their network. You can approach even complete strangers and make connections that will be of value to you both.

The Mental Barriers to Power Connecting

> At one time, our friends were just strangers to us. What if, as we pass all of the "strangers" in our lives, we looked at these strangers as if they could be friends?
>
> —JAMES A. MURPHY, *THE WAVES OF LIFE*

Unfortunately, for many people—including me—the power connector mindset is far from natural. As a young woman, I was shy, socially awkward, and something of an introvert. (When I read Susan Cain's book *Quiet: The Power of Introverts in a World That Can't Stop Talking*, I discovered that one-third to one-half of the U.S. population—including some of the highest-performing CEOs—are fundamentally introverts.[1]) Whenever I had to go to a group meeting for work, I would hide in the corner. But eventually my desire to further my career forced me to look at what was holding me back. It was clear that parts of my mindset had created shyness and reluctance to connect with others, so I worked hard to overcome those tendencies. I forced myself to talk to strangers. I made it a game: anybody I saw, I would figure out a way to talk to him or her. I came to believe that 95 percent of people on the earth would probably be happy to talk to me, and the other 5 percent I probably didn't want to know. The more I talked to people, the easier it became, and the freer I felt.

Since that time, whenever I talk to others who tell me they don't like "networking," I hear some of the same beliefs that I used to have that got in my way. I want to bring up the ones that seem to hold people back, and to offer "fixes" that might make connecting easier.

"I'm shy."

According to Susan Cain, there's a difference between being shy and being introverted. Introverts prefer environments that are not overly stimulating. They tend to maintain a circle of close friends, family, and colleagues. They can engage with others, but then they may need to retreat for a while to soothe their senses. On the other hand, shy people have a painful fear of social disapproval or humiliation that keeps them from engaging in the first place. Introverts may go to a conference and after a while wish they were back at the office. Shy people are too afraid to go to the conference in the first place, or they go, speak to no one, and leave as quickly as possible. For introverts, being power connectors can be okay as long as they can have some "quiet time." For shy people, meeting a lot of strangers and then connecting them to other people is their idea of hell. They're so afraid of saying or doing the wrong thing that they'd rather avoid social contact altogether, no matter how important or beneficial that contact might be.

The fix: You don't have to be an extrovert; you just have to engage. If you are really painfully shy, you may want to consult a counselor or coach to help you overcome any issues that may be holding you back. For the rest of us introverts with a tendency toward shyness, we need to develop enough courage and confidence to step out of our comfort zones and connect with those we don't know. Film producer Elizabeth Dell calls this "putting her face on." She has to spend a lot of time at industry events where the primary focus is meeting other professionals and networking to find out about potential new projects and collaborators. The atmosphere can be very competitive; "I try to remember that everyone else is also awkward and unsure and looking to meet people too," she says.

The other suggestion that often works is to emulate someone whose connecting skills you admire. Act as if you are not shy or introverted. Act as if you have all the confidence in the world. The more you act "as if," the more comfortable you will be and the less acting you will be doing.

And remember, the person you're connecting with may be just as shy and introverted as you.

"I'm self-conscious."

Self-consciousness is fear or nervousness caused when we focus on ourselves. According to psychology professors Thomas Gilovich, Victoria Husted Medvec, and Kenneth Savitsky, this apprehension is due to the all-too-human tendency to magnify the significance we have in the minds of others—the so-called *spotlight effect*.[2] Self-conscious individuals often feel they don't fit in; they are afraid that people are judging them for their appearance, status, or the way they talk or laugh—any of a dozen reasons. The problem is that by focusing on themselves instead of others, self-conscious people lose the ability to connect with anyone in a genuine manner.

The fix: Be other focused. In the mid-1990s, social psychologist James Pennebaker conducted a study that showed whenever people have the chance to talk about themselves, they feel better about and closer to the people with whom they're speaking.[3] Taking the focus off of yourself and putting it on the other person makes connecting much easier for you, and it makes the other person feel good. Engage with people by asking them to talk about what's important to them in their lives and businesses; create an "other focused" conversation.

"Strangers equal danger."

"Don't talk to strangers." How many of us had that burned into our brains when we were children—even though statistically it's the people we know who are more likely to do us harm?[4] While it is completely appropriate advice when we are four, five, or ten years old, a reluctance to engage with strangers will prevent you from finding some of your most important relationships.

The fix: Every important contact you have was once a stranger. Strangers equal opportunity. The ability to approach strangers with the purpose of connecting for your business is a critical skill. A 2012 survey of U.S. and U.K. networking behavior showed that small business owners met and talked with strangers (that is, potential customers) in bars and restaurants (38 percent), at the gym (23 percent), and on airplanes (17 percent). Of the business owners surveyed, 90 percent attributed at least some new business to this activity, with one-third saying it had brought in "a lot" of new business.[5] Strangers are often the key to lucky breaks and synchronicity. "If you're always hanging with the same tribe, you'll always think the same thoughts," writes Silicon Valley entrepreneur and speaker Nilofer Merchant. "I allot 20 percent of my annual budget for what I call 'serendipity creation,' ... new ideas, new people, new connections."[6]

Talking to strangers on airplanes can lead to great conversations—and occasionally produce key business connections as well. On a recent flight the young couple next to me had a very happy baby, who decided she needed to sit on my lap and play with my BlackBerry. Her parents and I started chatting, and the dad told me he runs a real estate investment fund in San Diego. In the course of our conversation he gave me some stellar advice on how to attract more money into a new VC fund (I was on its advisory board), and he agreed to get on the phone with our fund manager.

On another occasion I was able to be the "friendly stranger" to a man and his dad who were coming to Utah to hike in Zion National Park. We struck up a conversation on the flight, and the man told me they were both from Silicon Valley, and he had been a VP of a wealth management fund. I told him that I wished I had learned earlier how to monetize the money between my ears, and I asked if he had considered sitting on start-up company boards. "Only not-for-profits," he replied. I suggested that if he were to target a high-potential start-up, he could get 1.5 to 3 percent equity in the company for his contacts and knowledge. I could see the wheels turning in his mind, and before we left the plane, he asked for my card.

There are many wonderful souls in this world that sadly pass like ships in the night, not realizing what they are missing by not offering a kind word or a smile to a stranger. Whenever people tell me they hate talking with strangers, I start my reply by saying, "I was a stranger five seconds ago, and you're talking to me!" Then I suggest that they make it a game, as I did. I tell them to talk to three strangers in a day—starting with people who are "trapped" next to them in a grocery line, at the bank, or on a plane—and identify three things they have in common with each of them. "You'll find that most people are very gracious and friendly," I tell them. "They're delighted to talk and think that you made their day. If not, well, you'll probably never see them again anyway, so no harm, no foul. And you will have started to develop a stronger 'connection muscle.'"

"Networking is manipulative."

I agree—most "old school" networking is manipulative because the model is based on people using one another for their own gain. It focuses on what people can get out of relationships rather than what they can give.

The fix: Don't network. Connect. I wrote this book precisely because I *don't* like or believe in traditional networking. I want people to understand how to build great relationships that are based more on adding value to others than getting things for yourself. With the power connector approach, you'll feel good about the relationships you develop, and you'll find that you'll also receive far more because your connections want to help you.

"I have nothing to offer others."

If you have trouble with this, you're not alone. When I ask people to come up with a list of their accomplishments, most are hard-pressed to think of more than five.

The fix: Create a victory log of your accomplishments, no matter how small. First, you should recognize that you have an incredible number of ways that you can add value to other people. You may have the exact connection or resource they need, or a specific piece of information that can make all the difference for them. But you also have intrinsic value that you must acknowledge before you can connect effectively. You have a myriad of experiences and inherent qualities that are your gifts to the world; you just have to own them.

To create your list of experiences and qualities, come up with what I call a *victory log:* write down 50 things you have accomplished in your life. It can be big or little events from childhood to present day. My list includes: "Getting a D in geometry so I didn't flunk out of high school." "The first time I made $30,000." "The first speech I ever gave—it was at a Chamber of Commerce in Idaho; I was terrified, but I made it through." "Being appointed to the board of directors for MVRMC by the county commissioners." "My first trip to India." Do your best to put at least 50 accomplishments in your victory log, and then read all 50 items once a day. It will prepare you to know exactly what you have to offer when you power connect.

"They won't like me."

Usually this belief is rooted in fear and lack of self-esteem. People are afraid of what others will think of them and worried that, for whatever reason, they won't be good enough for others to like them. They go into any meeting looking for the ways other people are nicer to others, or cut them off, or simply don't treat them as well as they think they should be treated.

The fix: If *you* like others, they're likely to reciprocate. But make respect a requirement of any relationship. As humans, we tend to want to be liked by everyone we meet. However, this is impossible. No matter how great you are, not everyone will like you, often for reasons that have nothing to do with your likability. You may remind someone of a hated teacher, or you are seen as a rival or threat, or maybe someone was just having a bad day when you met.

You can't be liked by everyone, so don't try. Instead, try these three strategies. First, if you like others, they are usually more open to liking you back. Focus on whatever you like or admire in others; pretend that they could become your best friends. Second, if you have to be in a relationship with someone who doesn't like you, make your peace with his or her attitude—but at the same time, demand mutual respect. Power connectors may have to deal with bad actors (see Chapter 2) from time to time, and these people often don't like anybody, or they tend to be difficult or unpleasant. There is no purpose to being liked by such people, but as long as you have their respect, you are more likely to be able to relate to them on equal footing.

Third, don't ever violate your values simply to be liked. Power connectors understand that sometimes they are going to have to say no or take what might be an unpopular position, and they have to be okay with doing that. I've said no to many a deal offered by friend and stranger alike. In each case I articulate the reasons why I don't think it's a good fit, and I often point the person in a new direction. People generally come away from this with a positive experience because I have given their request due consideration and tried to be helpful.

"I'll get rejected."

I see a lot of people who do nothing because they are afraid of making a mistake, or they are afraid of being rejected for any reason at all. They figure that other people will just say no, so why even try? But that's like being the kid in school who never asks someone out or never tries to join a group just because they *might* be rejected, and they end up miserable.

The fix: Yell "Next!" It's absolutely fine if people turn you down because there are many more people out there who will be happy to help. If you're looking for investors, there are literally millions of millionaires who need places to invest. Everyone has problems, and no one has everything they need, and we are all looking for solutions that can come only through other people. If someone rejects you, it just means it wasn't the right fit for the moment. Walk away, yell "Next!" and start looking for the right opportunity.

People sometimes tell me that connecting is something you either like or don't like; you either have a facility for developing relationships or you don't. I reply that I've heard the same thing about leadership: it's something you're either born knowing how to do, or you'll never be good at it. But scientists studying leadership and genetics found that, while approximately 24 to 30 percent of leadership ability is inborn, the other 60 to 76 percent comes from environment and training.[7] In other words, leadership can be learned, and the same is true of connecting. With the right mindset, and an understanding of the foundation of a great relationship, everyone can build strong, mutually beneficial connections with anyone they wish.

The Basis of Every Power Connection

> The "luckiest" men and women are those whose personalities
> draw people to them and who have taken the time and
> trouble to build strong relationships with others.
> **—MAX GUNTHER, *THE LUCK FACTOR***

For power connectors, every relationship must be based on three elements: people must *know you, like you,* and *trust you.* For people to *know* you, you must get out of your comfort zone and into the right rooms, the right places, and the right ecosystems. As CareerFuel.net founder and CEO AnnMarie McIlwain commented, "Leave the office and circulate. Breathe the air of other people and cross-pollinate. As a former boss once said to me 'You never get dumb talking to people.'" Join groups on LinkedIn. Go to conferences. Volunteer for projects and committees in your industry and community. The only way people will know you is if you start showing up where they are.

"Knowing you" also means developing a compelling way of introducing yourself and what you do. In Chapter 6, "Phase 1: Prepare to Power Connect," you'll learn how to create an interesting, genuine summary (*not* an elevator speech) of what makes you and your business unique that can be tailored to be relevant to different people that you meet.

Once you are in the right places and you've made yourself known, you need to create a friendly and warm relationship—people need to *like* you. In 2007, psychology and organizational management professors Susan Fiske, Amy Cuddy, and Peter Glick did a study of how two key traits, warmth and competence (described as "the two universal dimensions of human social cognition), interact. While both are important, warmth was assessed before competence, and it carried more weight when it came to our relationships. This "reflects the importance of assessing other people's intentions before determining their ability to carry out those intentions," Fiske, Cuddy, and Glick wrote.[8] Of course, power connectors must demonstrate both warmth and competence, but I would argue that warmth and liking are the factors that create an initial good impression and a higher possibility of longer-term connections.

For people to like you, you must engage with them. Ask questions, and listen to the answers. Provide value in the moment (a contact name, a suggestion, or even a good joke or story can provide value), and then you do something to indicate you wish to continue the relationship (ask for a business card and give yours, give your LinkedIn information, and so on). In Chapter 7 you'll learn three golden questions that will make it very easy for you to engage with anyone you meet.

Once you keep your commitment to follow up, you are starting to develop the final essential characteristic of a power connection: *trust*. While liking can be created in one meeting, trust is a result of many little actions through time, commitments made and kept. As author Iyanla Vanzant says, "What breaks trust is when you don't do what you say you're going to do when you say you're going to do it. Love will endure, but trust is fragile." Marketing experts Mark E. McKinney and Amber Benson describe trust in a brand as being built upon the "three Cs"—credibility, care, and competence[9]—and the same is true of trust in an individual. With every commitment you keep, every phone call you return within 24 hours, every article you send, or small (or large) favor you do, your *credibility* rises, your *competence* is demonstrated, and your *caring* is felt.

Building Relationships Intelligently and for the Long Term

> "Networking" is yucky—but meeting cool people and
> being open with introducing others to your
> folks is fun and exciting.
>
> **—JASON BEST, COFOUNDER AND PRINCIPAL OF
> CROWDFUND CAPITAL ADVISORS**

The power connectors I know are very savvy about the relationships they build. Here's what I have found to be true of the mindsets of the best power connectors.

Power connectors connect for a reason.

Don't just connect for the sake of being able to say, "My Rolodex is bigger than yours." Remember the 5+50+100 model? You don't need thousands of connections, just the 155 that are right for you. Power connectors focus on the quality of their relationships, not the quantity. (I define quality relationships as those with integrity, competence, and character.) That doesn't mean you should connect only with those who you think are useful. Movers and shakers in any field are particularly sensitive to those who are, as Adam Grant calls them, "takers," who are only out for what they can gain from others. The reason you connect should be to *give* something or to create mutual benefit. Power connectors look to build relationships that can provide great benefit for all parties concerned.

Power connectors connect for real.

Power connectors know that any relationship they seek to develop needs to be based on genuinely connecting with and caring for the other person. Recently Iyanla Vanzant said to me, "We have to be care-full, full of care, no matter what the relationship is. I care about you, your needs, who you are, and what you bring to the table. Caring is at the core of all relationships." Do your best to find things to like in others. Develop an insatiable curiosity about other people—who they are, what they need, and what motivates them. Most power connectors I know are endlessly fascinated by the incredible diversity of human nature and endlessly interested in the marvels that human beings can create.

Power connectors connect for the long term.

Just as the money you invest today will grow through the years, the investments you make in connecting with others will grow and pay dividends in the future. Once you develop those genuine, solid relationships, you don't have to see or talk with your connections every day; they will be there for you when you need them. I have people in my network that I haven't talked to for perhaps six months to a year, but they will take my call or the call of someone I recommend.

Power connectors also understand that, while some relationships end, it's in everyone's best interest that they end as well as possible. A fellow angel investor comments, "I've definitely seen the 'don't burn any bridges' rule come in handy—you never know when you'll need to reach out to that person who, just a short while ago, you thought you'd never speak with again." If someone drifts out of your network or you part with them for any other reason, always think long term when it comes to the way you end the connection.

Power connectors connect through the levels.

Every connection is an entry into a new personal ecosystem of potentially important contacts. Film producer Elizabeth Dell is part of a world based almost exclusively on the power of connecting your connections with others. "I try to make a practice of always asking new people what they are working on, what they are looking for, and what they need. And if I encounter opportunities for someone else, I pass it along," she reports. "Every time I share an opportunity, I build a connection and a friendship." Power connectors with extensive, high-quality networks understand *leverage*: while they might not have the answers or resources you need, other people in their network will—and their value is to serve as the conduit that connects you with those people.

Power connectors treat everyone well.

When you enter the world of power connecting, you meet a lot of people—and you never know if the guy handing you a name tag at an industry meeting might turn out to be the company CEO in 15 to 20 years, or if the woman who calls you out of the blue for an interview can put you in touch with your next source of funding. While power connectors are judicious about whom they put into their 5+50+100, they are smart enough to treat everyone they encounter as a valued and valuable human being.

In fact, many power connectors specialize in mentoring those who are on their way up. Even though he's incredibly busy with his own start-up, Lee Blaylock helped to get the Dallas chapter of Startup Grind (a Silicon Valley–based group that works to educate, inspire, and connect entrepreneurs worldwide) up and running. "I know that I have built a good reputation for helping people, and that reputation has benefited me when I go to other people and ask for assistance, coaching, or introductions," he says.

Power connectors add value first.

No matter how successful, everyone needs help in some way. The bank president may need a good batting coach for his son, for instance, or the VC fund manager may be delighted to hear about your friend's start-up. Seeking to add value *first* is a prominent feature of all power connector relationships. It's "the law of reciprocity": when you give of yourself—your time, your effort, your connections—to help someone else, they naturally want to reciprocate. "Think about how you can support the work of others and spread their messages," writes Ellia Communications founder and *Forbes* blogger Kathy Caprino. "When you come from a place of service (instead of thinking of 'me, me, me'), help and support is returned to you a hundredfold."

THE POWER CONNECTING
SYSTEM

....

If the industrial era was about building things,
the social era is about connecting things,
people, and ideas.

—NILOFER MERCHANT, AUTHOR,
ENTREPRENEUR, AND VISIONARY

With a power connector's mindset, building a powerful network will be easier, but you still need to find and prioritize your connections and manage them for maximum impact. For that, you will need a combination of the right strategy, the right skills, and the right information.

Power connection can be broken down into four phases, with specific steps in each phase. In Phase 1, you prepare to connect by analyzing yourself and your current network and determining the people you need to add (and from which ecosystems) to make your power circles wider, deeper, and more robust.

In Phase 2, you plan your first contact with new individuals by preparing a *share, value-add*, and *ask*. Then you ready yourself to connect immediately with the people you meet. Finally, you add value quickly and strengthen the relationship from the start.

Phase 3 is about assessment and consolidation: you do something to reconnect within 24 hours, evaluate the connection and place it within your 5+50+100 circles, then deepen the relationship by continuing to add value.

Phase 4 is where the real power of power connecting resides: connecting people within your network for their (and your) greater success.

These four phases will lead you from the first meeting to creating deep, quality relationships of mutual value.

Remember, the *right* relationships, in the *right* ecosystems, created and nurtured in the *right* way, will accelerate your success.

6

Phase 1: Prepare to Power Connect

Luck is a matter of preparation
meeting opportunity.

—SENECA

O nce you have the power connector mindset, building strategic relationships will take a combination of self-knowledge, strategy, skills, and above all, preparation. To establish the foundation for high-quality connections, you will be examining every aspect of yourself and your current network and then creating a clear and compelling plan to maximize your relationships, both the ones you have and the ones you will make.

Preparation consists of three parts: getting clear on what you have to offer and what you need; evaluating your current network and putting your contacts into 5+50+100 power circles; and creating a plan to reach out to new relationships based on (1) shared values, (2) added value, and (3) value created together. In this chapter you'll go through a process of capturing (on paper or on your computer, tablet, or phone) everything you will need to be ready to connect with the right people, in the right places, in the right ways to create the right relationships for your personal and professional life.

Part 1: Know Who You Are, What You Have to Offer, and What You Need

> The most important factor in making your connections
> work exponentially well is knowing yourself.
>
> —WINSTON PEREZ, FOUNDER, CONCEPT MODELING

With power connecting, much of the value you will provide people will be your ability to connect them with resources they need. However, at the center of your 5+50+100 power circles is *you*, so you must assess your own value as a connection. You must be willing to declare your own strengths and accomplishments, for they are at the core of what you will be able to offer others. Everything—from your time playing baseball to your expertise in computer games to your having found the best preschool for your child—may be exactly the value that someone else needs. Sometimes the most valuable things you can provide are a smile, a listening ear, and a caring heart.

You also must be willing to be honest about your weaknesses and what you need from others. According to influence expert Robert Cialdini, the strongest relationships are built not on one-sided value but on the ability for both members to be able to contribute to the other.[1] Just as you must be able to identify the deficiencies and needs in your business so you can fill them efficiently, you must be able to identify the weaknesses and deficiencies in yourself and your network so you can compensate for weaknesses and fill any holes in your existing power circles.

In this step you'll assemble a range of information that you'll use when you begin mapping your past and future strategic relationships. I suggest that you create a chart for this information; you'll want a lot of flexibility when it comes to using the data later. (You can download forms for all the steps in this book at http://www.judyrobinett.com/resources.)

Let's start by listing your accomplishments.

Step 1: Make a list of all of your professional and personal accomplishments and associations, and the ecosystems they have allowed you to enter.

The professional list (see Table 6.1) is similar to a résumé or CV. It also should indicate where each of these accomplishments took place (for example, the

Table 6.1 Professional Accomplishments

Association	Accomplishment	Ecosystems
Indiana University	Degree in business	Community Academic Industry
XYZ Corporation	Promoted to brand manager in 3 years	Industry
Brands Unlimited	Founded my own company	Industry Community
Brands Unlimited	Raised $500,000 in capital for my business	Financial
Sarah Ross political campaign	Ran entrepreneur fundraising efforts	Political Financial Industry
Young Presidents' Organization (YPO)	Member; elected to finance committee	Industry

Table 6.2 Personal Accomplishments

Association	Accomplishment	Ecosystems
High school track team	Captain	Community
Big Brother	Mentored an 11-year-old	Community Charitable
XYZ Corporation	Ran the company's yearly fundraising campaign for breast cancer research	Community Charitable
My child's school	Organized and chaperoned a class trip to Washington, DC	Community Political Family and friends
Big Brother fund-raising campaign	Chair of annual city campaign	Charitable Financial Industry

schools you attended, the companies where you have worked, the professional organizations to which you have belonged, and the awards you have received). The personal list (see Table 6.2) includes everything from church affiliation to charitable organizations, sports teams, community groups, and academic networks. Both lists should include the ecosystems in which these accomplishments took place—family, community, industry, finance, politics, and so on. (If you did a victory log as I suggested in the last chapter, you can use it as a starting point.) These associations and ecosystems provide access to potential networks of connection and places, as well as ways to add value, and your accomplishments are indications of your strengths and skills (see Step 2).

The associations and ecosystems to which you have belonged can be the sources of some of your most important connections. Even if it's been years since you were in touch with your college friends, people from your first job, or your parents' neighbors, you never know where these contacts will lead. Entrepreneur and top *Forbes* blogger Devin Thorpe says that his most important business relationship was with someone whose lawn he mowed as a teenager. Years later, when Devin moved back to Salt Lake City, the neighbor, who was CFO of one of Utah's largest companies, hired Devin. Keep your list handy when it comes to identifying people to add to your power circles because you may find candidates in these ecosystems and in past associates' networks. You'll also use this list to assess your skills and strengths.

Step 2: To assess your value-add potential, make an inventory of your skills, knowledge, and strengths.

Every individual possesses a unique mixture of abilities, information, and experience that creates value for others. Take an objective look at your professional and personal lists. What do you have to offer that others might need or want? What skills and strengths do you possess? One of the easiest ways to create this inventory is to look at your personal and professional accomplishments and, next to each one, write the skills, knowledge, and strengths that you demonstrated or learned from it. For an example, see Table 6.3.

Skills and knowledge come from many different areas including finance, management, teambuilding, computers and social media, negotiations, communication, sales, and writing. Strengths are more personal qualities and innate talents such as being disciplined, having mathematical ability, being able to put people at ease, being willing to take risks, being a team player, and being a good leader. (If you would like an extensive list of personal qualities, see *Now, Discover Your Strengths* by Marcus Buckingham and Donald Clifton.) What skills do you possess that could be of value to a strategic connection? What strengths make you a great colleague, leader, manager, organizer, or

Table 6.3 Skills, Knowledge, and Strengths Inventory

Accomplishment	Skill or Knowledge	Strength
On high school track team	Teamwork; learned to do numbers in my head when figuring out split times	Discipline Perseverance
Ran my company's yearly fundraising campaign for breast cancer research	Managed a large budget Communications Sales (had to sell my ideas to management)	Good with numbers Good at marketing Great at assembling teams Leadership
Raised $500,000 in capital for my business	Created a great business plan Sales (convinced investors to invest) Budgeting	Perseverance Leadership Assembled a great team Numbers

mentor? Ask three to five of your closest associates what they believe are your greatest strengths, and look for patterns and commonalities in their responses. As in the previous table, you may see that some of your skills, knowledge, or strengths will carry over from one accomplishment to another. This is common: as we develop our strengths and skills, we're called on to use them in different contexts and ecosystems.

Believing that you have something valuable to offer is a critical step in creating strategic relationships. This is a time to put your best foot forward. If you're willing to put yourself on the line, ask the people you consider your closest personal and professional contacts to give you their perspective. Not long ago I made this suggestion to Mary Kopczynski, CEO of Eight of Nine Consulting. Afterward she told me, "Some of my friends responded as I expected: 'You make things happen,' 'You get stuff done,' 'You accomplish what you put your mind to,' and so on. But then my best friend, a super busy doctor and mother of two, wrote me the most *incredible* statement. She said I am unparalleled in my ability to diagnose a problem, produce three creative ideas for overcoming that particular obstacle, assess their strengths and weaknesses, make a decision about the best course of action, and then get it done. You said I would be astounded by the answers, and you were right."

Often other people can see our strengths and skills more clearly than we can. After she graduated from college, Janet Hanson was running the pro shop at St. Andrew's Golf Club in her home town of Hastings-on-Hudson in New York. One day Dan Crowley, who was a neighbor in Hastings, walked in and told her, "You're too smart to work here."

"I didn't plan on going to business school, nor did I ever think about having a career in finance," she remembers. "However, two very powerful men in finance told me I would be crazy not to go for it, so I did." Janet became one of the first women on the fixed income trading floor at Goldman Sachs.

Once you have your list, mark the skills and strengths that you most enjoy using. Most of us are very good at many different things, but there are some that light us up. These are our passions, and the more we can exercise these for the service of others as well as our own benefit, the happier and more productive we will be. These skills and strengths also allow you to stand out from others in your field or area, and they will help you build connections with others. As angel investor Martin Zwilling wrote in *Forbes*, "Every entrepreneur has personal knowledge and strengths which can get them past the social level in connection. These should include professional position, existing relationships, specific expertise, professional appearance, and passion for your cause or business. Use them effectively."[2]

Another list we need to make, however, indicates the areas where we may need help.

Step 3: List your weaknesses and your deficiencies in skills and knowledge. What do you need to improve personally and professionally? What do you need to learn or add?

There's a concept in psychology called the *Johari window*.[3] It's a grid that's designed to map self-awareness. There are four quadrants, as shown in Table 6.4.

Hopefully the skills, knowledge, and strengths you described are part of your public self—what you and others can see easily. And no one can truly know what your potential is, although I believe that strategic relationships often help bring out more of that potential. What you need to examine in this task, however, are the private self and blind self quadrants.

Table 6.4 The Johari Window

	What You See in Me	What You Do Not See in Me
What I See in Me	Public self	Private, hidden self
What I Do Not See in Me	Blind self (my blind spots)	Undiscovered, unknown self (my potential)

Each of us has a private self that we choose not to disclose to the world at large. That's to be expected; we don't want to fall into the modern-day TMI (too much information) trap of bringing too much of our deeply personal lives into our businesses. But if you are holding back some of your skills and abilities, or hiding your strengths because you don't recognize how valuable they are, or you have self-esteem issues, or you don't want to "brag" about yourself—*stop*. A key to power connecting is to recognize the value you have to give to others. You need to be willing to bring your skills, knowledge, and strengths out into the open and let others know what you have to offer. Otherwise, you'll be cheating them and yourself.

It's also very possible that you have managed to hide many of your personal and professional deficiencies in the private self quadrant. After all, no one wants to put their weaknesses on parade, and if you can compensate for a lack of sales skills by hiring someone to handle sales for you, for example, so much the better. However, if you're hiding a weakness to keep from addressing it, then you're only holding yourself back from getting the help that might make all the difference.

Make a list of the things you're not good at, the stuff you hate to do, the areas where you *know* you are deficient in skills, knowledge, ability, or interest. This can be either personal or professional. Next to each, write some ideas for skills or knowledge that could help you with this, and/or the strengths you could work on developing to make this better. For an example, see Table 6.5.

You can gain skills and knowledge in four ways. First, you can *acquire* it yourself. If it's of interest to you and you want to plunge into learning about a particular kind of software, for example, or if you want to discover the ins and outs of venture capital, go for it. However, if it's a skill or piece of knowledge

Table 6.5 Skills, Knowledge, and Strengths to Develop

Weakness or Deficiency	What *Skill or Knowledge* Do I Need to Acquire, Hire, or Connect To?	What *Strength* Do I Need to Develop?
Raising money—I have trouble asking for the amount I want.	Negotiation skills Writing a better business plan and budgeting so I can make my case	Assertiveness Self-confidence The "ask"
Overwhelmed—I always feel like there is too much to do.	Time management Delegation	Organization Prioritization Ability to leave the office when I leave the office

that you are not particularly interested in but you still recognize its importance, you may be able to *hire* it. For example, you need to write a business plan for your next start-up. You have a great vision and super partners, but you are weak when it comes to projecting the costs of manufacturing overseas. You can hire an expert to be part of your team, or you can simply employ him or her to provide you with the information you need. Third, you can *barter* for it: "I'll help you with this if you'll help me with that." Exchanging value is a great strategy (although, as you'll see in later chapters, I believe you should add enough value first so that the other person is eager to help).

The fourth path to gain the skill or knowledge is through a relationship or *connection*—one you already have or one you will seek to develop. Suppose that for your latest product, you want to try a social media campaign to rev up sales. Instead of asking your already overtaxed marketing department to come up with something new, you put out a request to your LinkedIn network for possible resources. Within two days you have multiple names of recommended consultants and services to bid on your social media needs.

Admitting that we lack certain skills and knowledge is one thing. Owning up to strengths that we lack is usually harder, especially since we're often unaware of them in the first place—they're in our blind spot. However, it's important that we become cognizant of these issues so they don't get in the way of our strategic relationships. One of the easiest ways to discover blind spots is to ask people you trust for their feedback. A simple question like "What's one thing you think I could improve?" may give you a good idea of where you need to focus your efforts. (Don't be surprised if some of those weaknesses and deficiencies you thought were private show up here; we're usually not as good at hiding them as we think.) One of the great secrets of power connecting lies in the ability to humbly acknowledge our weaknesses and failings. It gives evidence of our common humanity, and it opens the door for others to be of assistance (which makes for stronger relationships). It keeps the ego in check, and it gives the people we meet the chance to be human themselves. More important, it creates an atmosphere of honesty and self-awareness that is fundamental to all great relationships.

In the next step, it's time to think aspirationally.

Step 4: What skills, knowledge, and strengths would you like to add or develop for your personal and professional growth?

Even if we have a great list of accomplishments, skills, knowledge, and strengths and few weaknesses, we need to keep learning and growing to keep from falling behind. What skills and knowledge do you already have that you need to keep improving? Technology is changing every day, and business situations can turn on a dime. What are you doing to keep abreast of your field? What skills and knowledge would you like to add that would help you either personally or professionally? Make sure to add some personal skills and knowledge, as they will enrich your professional life and connections as well.

Make a list of the additional strengths you would like to cultivate, remembering that certain strengths are universally valued. Such a list would include honesty, courage, flexibility, modesty, generosity, empathy, passion, kindness, humor, likability, integrity, trustworthiness, self-confidence, curiosity, a drive for excellence, altruism, perseverance, respect, boldness, accountability, openness, helpfulness, willingness to take risks, and a commitment to being a lifelong learner. Every skill and piece of knowledge has the potential to make you better in your profession and your life; but any strength that you incorporate will make you a better human being first and foremost.

Part 2: Develop and Implement Your 5+50+100 System

Call it a clan, call it a network, call it a tribe, call it a family:
whatever you call it, whoever you are, you need one.
—JANE HOWARD, AUTHOR

Just as every publicly traded company creates quarterly financial reports and year-end financial statements to give investors an idea of the health of the business, you should evaluate the status of your network regularly to determine its health and fitness. And you must have some kind of system for capturing and categorizing the members of your network and the ways you stay in touch with them. Laura Leist, author of *Eliminate the Chaos at Work: 25 Techniques to Increase Productivity*, is an expert on customer relationship management (CRM) software for business. She writes, "Although a CRM is an investment of both time and money, your ROI here will far outweigh the costs of doing nothing. But before you hastily jump in and purchase any software, you need to analyze your business processes. You must understand how you want to use the data you capture and what output you want from the software."[4] This understanding of how to capture and use data will be key as you set up your own personal CRM system.

Mike Muhney, who founded ACT! and, more recently, VIPorbit, commented, "People need a system that meets the needs of the world we live in, where we're operating on multiple devices and the line between business and personal connections is blurred. I have golfing buddies who are also customers, strategic allies, and investors, so I want to be able to keep track of how we interact in multiple orbits." As you prepare to organize your connections, find a system that works for you. (I've put a list of potential CRM and networking resources in the back of this book. However, technology and software are changing all the time, so any recommendations I might make are time sensitive.)

No matter what system you choose, use it in Step 5 to create a list of the people in your network right now.

Step 5: Make a list of your current connections.

This list includes everyone in your phone, in your Rolodex, in your Outlook program, or anywhere else that you keep contact information. Look at your

LinkedIn connections, Facebook friends—anyone with whom you are currently connected in any way—and his or her role in your life. Make this list comprehensive: everyone from your local Starbucks barista to your dry cleaner, children's babysitter, the IT consultant for your firm, mechanic, accountant, minister, printer, and the attendant at the golf club or health spa who knows your name. (As you remember from Chapter 2, such distant connections are weak links that can lead to productive relationships.) If you put these names into a chart, you will be able to sort the list by any of a number of different categories, which will make it easier to put them into your power circles.

Once you have this list, divide your contacts into personal, professional, or both. Then rate each connection as to importance and/or closeness to you by using a scale of 1 to 5, 1 being closest and 5 being just a casual acquaintance. Next, put a note next to each person's name to indicate the context of this connection: business, politics, charity, social friend, club, school, and so on. (You'll use this information to place each connection in the proper ecosystem.) Finally, note where each individual lives and/or works. Eventually you'll use these notes to assemble your 5+50+100 power circles.

Once you have the list of your current connections, look back at the professional and personal accomplishments and associations you created earlier. Should any of the people involved with those associations or accomplishments be added to the list of your current connections? If so, add them to your list. (See Table 6.6 for part of a sample grid.)

Putting this list together may take a while, but there are multiple benefits. First, you'll get an idea of how many connections you already have.

Second, you'll start to see how these connections are spread throughout the different areas of your life.

Third, you'll start to notice patterns. Do you have a lot of professional connections and few personal ones, or vice versa? Are almost all of your connections at the same professional level? Do you have connections among people who are just starting out? Do you have contacts with executives or entrepreneurs that are at a higher level than you by virtue of experience or success? Do you have a diverse circle of peers?

Table 6.6 Current Connections

Name	Role	Personal, Professional, or Both	Closeness (1=Close, 5=Casual)	Context	Location
Sue Smith	Business partner	Both	1	Business	Miami
Sam Travers	Spouse	Personal	1	Personal	Miami
Joe Peters	Minister	Personal	4	Church	Miami
Steve Feliz	Mentor	Both	1	Business; school	New York
Marvin Chin	Professor; mentor	Both	3	Grad school	Chicago
Patty Nathan	VC funder	Professional	2	Business; money	San Jose
Howard Finn	Kids' teacher	Personal	4	School	Miami
Mark Starr	College roommate	Personal	2	School	Australia
Alice King	Local council rep	Professional	5	Political	Miami
Chuck Ames	Golf buddy; client	Both	3	Business; golf	Miami
Radha Shrinavas	Banker	Professional	2	Business; money	Miami
Bob Miller	Admin assistant	Professional	2	Business	Miami
George Arica	Next door neighbor	Personal	3	Neighbor-hood	Miami
Claudio Vero	Supplier	Professional	4	Business	Italy
Carl Peterson	Mows our lawn	Personal	5	Home	Miami

Fourth, you'll start to see the interconnections between the people you know. Your minister may know your banker, for instance, or your mentor and one of your investors may be part of the same professional association.

Fifth, and most important, each of the people on your list has a network of contacts that is as large if not larger than yours. Once you begin to understand your network and your place in it, you can be better positioned to take advantage of all that these connections have to offer. Remember, *wherever you want to go, relationships will get you there.*

Step 6: From your current connections, choose your Top 5, Key 50, and Vital 100.

When you look at your list of connections, your Top 5 should be easy to identify: they are usually close family and friends, including business associates whom you consider close friends. (You probably rated them 1 in closeness.) In this group, your personal and professional lives will overlap; it's important to have connections of both kinds in your inner circle.

Your Key 50 are friends and associates whom you know you can call upon for all kinds of help and advice, and vice versa. Stephen R. Covey calls this group your "circle of influence"; if your Key 50 is solid, you will have access to many of the resources you need. Usually these people would be ranked a 2 or 3 in terms of closeness, but they can have different roles and be from different contexts in your life. Your college roommate who now lives on the other side of the country but whom you call and ask for professional advice could be one of your Key 50, for example, as could the banker who gave you your first business loan and still handles your account.

Your Vital 100 are often the relationships that you ranked 4 in closeness (some of them may be a 5, but it's unlikely that you'd put casual acquaintances in your Vital 100). This group should represent a wide diversity of locations, contexts, and roles. I'd suggest you see your Vital 100 as akin to athletes on the bench: you pay attention to them, add value to them, and regard them as important members of your team.

Take your list of connections, and in a separate column, place as many connections as you can in your Top 5, Key 50, and Vital 100 (see Table 6.7). Not everyone on your list will fit into the 5+50+100 power circles, and that's fine. Once you've categorized your connections into the different power circles, sort the list by category.

Table 6.7 Your Current Power Circles: Top 5, Key 50, and Vital 100

Name	Role	Personal, Professional, or Both	Closeness (1=Close, 5=Casual)	Context	Location	Power Circle
Sue Smith	Business partner	Both	1	Business	Miami	Top 5
Sam Travers	Spouse	Personal	1	Personal	Miami	Top 5
Steve Feliz	Mentor	Both	1	Business	New York	Top 5
Mark Starr	College roommate	Personal	2	School	Australia	Key 50
Marvin Chin	Professor; mentor	Both	3	Grad school	Chicago	Key 50
Patty Nathan	VC funder	Professional	2	Business; money	San Jose	Key 50
Chuck Ames	Friend; golf buddy; client	Both	3	Business; golf	Miami	Key 50
Radha Shrinavas	Banker	Professional	2	Business; money	Miami	Key 50
Bob Miller	Admin assistant	Professional	2	Business	Miami	Key 50
George Arica	Next door neighbor	Personal	3	Neighbor-hood	Miami	Key 50
Joe Peters	Minister	Personal	4	Church	Miami	Vital 100
Howard Finn	Kids' teacher	Personal	4	School	Miami	Vital 100
Alice King	Local council rep	Professional	5	Political	Miami	Vital 100
Claudio Vero	Supplier	Professional	4	Business	Italy	Vital 100
Carl Peterson	Mows our lawn	Personal	5	Home	Miami	

How do you feel about your current 5+50+100 power circles? Why did you place people in those particular groups? Are your Top 5 and Key 50 the kind of people that you are proud and happy to have as part of your "circle of influence"? What value have you provided your power circles in the past? What value have they provided you? It's critical that you know what is important to your Key 50 so that you can keep your eyes open and ears to the ground for anything that will be of value to them. Even small value-adds will help to keep your connections with this group strong.

How healthy is your Vital 100? Does this group represent a diverse range of occupations, roles, locations, and relationships? How often are you in touch with these people, and are there some with whom you need to reconnect in order to revitalize the relationship? You should reach out to the members of this group at least once a month to maintain your connection, even at a distance. Remember, each person in your Vital 100 possesses his or her own network, and people in those networks are often the weak ties that lead to resources you could not access otherwise. Winston Perez tells a story of a top-level executive who found himself unemployed. Winston told him to print out and examine his "network database" of people he knew through his former job. The executive complained that he couldn't see much use in these contacts because they were not particularly close friends or colleagues. But one day, as the man was looking at the list, he saw the names of three people he had not been in touch with for a long time. He called them, and because of those calls, within three weeks he was offered a new, high-level position.

Finally, notice whether you have a lot of uncategorized connections. If so, are these relationships that you don't really need to focus on, or do you perhaps need to place *more* focus on them in order to move them into your Vital 100 or higher? As Nicholas Christakis and James Fowler remind us, "Social networks require tending. . . . While social networks are fundamentally and distinctively human, and ubiquitous, they should not be taken for granted."[5]

The 5+50+100 power circles will help keep your most important relationships organized, categorized, and nurtured. Will you have relationships outside of your power circles? Of course. Will people move in and out of your power circles through the years? Naturally. But using power circles will help you avoid the kind of "relationship overwhelm" that many people tell me they face when they receive yet another request from a LinkedIn contact or get handed 20 more business cards in the halls of an industry conference. And it will give you concrete guidelines for which relationships to nurture, and when, in order to keep all of your connections strong and healthy.

Part 3: Design the Power Circles You Need for Greater Success

> The types of people you choose to surround yourself with will ultimately define the caliber of person you will be. For this reason, it is critical to choose your mentors, associates, and close business confidantes wisely.
>
> —ANU BHARDWAJ, FOUNDER, VENTURE CATALYST PRIVATE EQUITY PARTNERS

You now have a map of your current power circles. But did you perhaps feel that there were some "holes" in your network, places where you could really use some additional relationship strength? You need to consciously design your power circles to include the people whom you can help and who can help you. Your goal is to create a streamlined group of 155 key relationships—people who share your values, with whom you will consistently connect, and to whom you will add value.

Step 7: Rate yourself and your current 5+50+100 in terms of resources and influence.

Add two columns to your power circles chart. In the first, write the resources this connection can access. In the second, on a scale of 1 to 5, rank the level of influence this connection has within his or her ecosystems. Influence can be everything from a position, a title, a network, a level of experience, or access. Someone like the secretary of the governor of a state, for example, may be a 4 due to his or her position, but he or she would be a 1 due to access. You need to do this for all of your connections; even the Vital 100 whom you contact only once a month may be a level 1 conduit to the precise resource you need.

And put yourself at the top of the chart. Because of your accomplishments and connections, you have your own influence level in the ecosystems where you are active. Rank yourself in each of the ecosystems. This will help you start to evaluate where you need more access and more help.

Table 6.8 shows an example of the addition of the Resource and Influence Score columns to the previous power circles chart.

If the people you know have great influence, you may not need to add to your current network. However, for most of us it is possible to increase

Table 6.8 Current Power Circles: Resources and Influence

Name	Role	Location	Ecosystem or Context	Power Circle	Resources	Influence Score
Me		Miami	Business Family Industry Community Financial Politics		Own business Relatives own their own businesses too United Way board Local council rep VC relationship YPO membership	Business 1 Family 1 Industry 4 Community 2 Financial 4 Politics 4
Sue Smith	Business partner	Miami	Industry Friends	Top 5	Business On board of industry association	3
Sam Travers	Spouse	Miami	Family	Top 5	Health care exec. Chair of parents' organization	2
Steve Feliz	Mentor	New York	Industry Friends	Top 5	New York industry network Media network	1
Mark Starr	College roommate	Australia	Friends	Key 50	Overseas network Real estate expert	3
Marvin Chin	Professor; mentor	Chicago	Industry Friends	Key 50	Academic network Industry network	1
Patty Nathan	VC funder	San Jose	Financial	Key 50	Financial network Access to funding Expansion advice	1
Chuck Ames	Friend; golf buddy; client	Miami	Business Friend	Key 50	Community bigwig Politically connected Charities	2

(continues)

Table 6.8 (cont.) Current Power Circles: Resources and Influence

Name	Role	Location	Ecosystem or Context	Power Circle	Resources	Influence Score
Radha Shrinavas	Banker	Miami	Business Financial	Key 50	Local financial connections National financial connections	2
Bob Miller	Admin assistant	Miami	Business	Key 50	Staff connections in business Church Volunteer	4
George Arica	Next door neighbor	Miami	Friends	Key 50	Real estate broker Kiwanis Arts connection	3
Joe Peters	Minister	Miami	Community	Vital 100	Church Community Charity	3
Howard Finn	Kids' teacher	Miami	Community	Vital 100	Community Sports Academic connections	4
Alice King	Local council rep	Miami	Political	Vital 100	Local politics Community Charitable	2
Claudio Vero	Supplier	Italy	Industry	Vital 100	Industry Overseas Financial	1

the power of our network simply by adding a few new people. Determining *which* new connections you wish to add, however, is more easily done within the context of specific goals.

Step 8: List three to five of your professional goals for the next three months, six months, and one year.

Watch the TV show *Shark Tank* and you'll see what can happen to entrepreneurs who aren't crystal clear about what they want and their plans to get there. If you don't know where you're going, a million contacts (or a million dollars) won't help. Truly successful people have specific targets they want to attain and actionable plans to achieve those goals. Then they can approach their connections with a specific, clear, and succinct "ask." Take a few minutes to write your top three to five goals for the next three months, six months, and one year in a new chart (see Table 6.9).

If it takes a village to raise a child, it takes a strong network to create success. What would make it possible for you to accomplish your goals more

Table 6.9 Professional Goals

Goal	Timeline
Bring in 4 new clients	3 months
Expand manufacturing capacity by 40 percent	6 months
Get venture capital funding for new plant overseas	1 year

easily? What can your current network do to be of assistance? And what additional help might you need?

Step 9: What help do you need to accomplish these goals? What people? Opportunities? Knowledge? Funding? What ecosystems do you need to access?

For each of your professional goals, you are going to create what I call a CRM—a *critical resource map*. (You can do this on a chart, or you can use a whiteboard and Post-it notes.) Put your goal at the top, and underneath it put four categories: *key people, opportunities, knowledge*, and *funding sources*. For each category, put the resources you already have access to through your power circles and their networks. Then, in separate columns, make note of the resources you still need, and possible connections to them in your current power circles. See Table 6.10 for an example of a critical resource map.

Now, look at the list of resources you need and who might have them. These two columns will tell you where you might need to expand your power circles.

Step 10: Whom do you need to add to your power circles to accomplish your short- and long-term goals?

It's hard to play baseball if you have only a pitcher and one fielder. It's also hard to play baseball if you only know swimmers. To accomplish your goals, you need to have the right connections. Springboard cofounder Amy Millman says, "I always advise people starting out to build their own personal advisory board with people they want to know and/or respect." You also need to ensure that you have enough connections in the right ecosystems. Look closely at the ecosystems in which your network is active. How much influence do your current "team members" have in their respective ecosystems? In which

Table 6.10 Critical Resource Map

Goal: Expand Manufacturing Capacity by 40 Percent			
	Resources I Have	Resources I Need	Who Might Have Them
Key people: Who's my who?	Sue, my business partner Steve, my mentor (he's run larger factories before) Lin, HR head Mike, salesperson for new equipment	New factory manager 10 new staff members Trainer for new workers	Marvin (mentor) Chuck (client) George (neighbor)
Key opportunities: Where's the right room and the right ecosystem?	Permits for factory expansion Community support for new jobs and new facility	Local council for permits Revision to community plan to allow for bigger plant Industry advice on issues with larger plants	Alice (council rep) Joe (minister) Claudio (supplier)
Key knowledge: What information do I need?	Training to support new equipment Tax and insurance implications of larger plant	Tax planning Equipment information Insurance information	Sam (accountant) Mike (equipment salesperson) Steve (mentor)
Key funding sources: Where's the money?	Local bank: great relationship for 20 years Other funding sources: explore selling part of company or taking on another partner	Larger branch bank for bigger loan to finance new equipment Look for investors or possible partners	Patty (VC funder) Radha (banker)

ecosystems would you like to increase your connections? Remember that the eight key ecosystems are family and friends, passions and interests, career or profession, government and politics, finance, media, industry, and community. Where do you need to connect with more individuals with greater influence?

Each ecosystem possesses a number of movers and shakers, and these people may or may not be visible to those outside or on the fringes of that particular ecosystem. In the world of high-tech venture capital, for instance, there are several people who are well known in Silicon Valley, like Tim Draper, Heidi Roizen, and Marc Andreessen. But dozens of other venture capitalists are unknown to outsiders; to gain access to them, you must know someone already inside the ecosystem.

If you wish to enter a particular ecosystem or increase your level of connections within it, start with the people in your power circles first. Suppose you have a thriving company manufacturing widgets in Dallas, Texas. One day a former associate calls and tells you about an abandoned manufacturing plant not far from where he lives in Atlanta, Georgia. "You could get this plant for a song and open up a second factory," he says. "Don't you have a lot of customers in the Southeast? You could cut your shipping costs by 50 percent and your labor costs by at least 25 percent." You're tempted—but Atlanta has its own political, financial, community, and industrial ecosystems, and the only person you know there is your former associate. So you call or e-mail your power circles to ask them about their connections in the Atlanta area. "If I were going to open a branch in Atlanta, whom would I need to know?" you ask.

Within a day or so, you start getting responses. "My mom lives in Atlanta, and she knows the mayor." "Here's the number of John Smith; he's in charge of institutional lending at Georgia's biggest bank. I'll e-mail him today to introduce you." "If you're doing manufacturing, you need to watch out for groundwater regulations. Keisha Abbott opened a plant not too far from Atlanta; give her a call, and she'll walk you through the pitfalls." "I've always heard that Marcia Waters is the one you need to see in Atlanta. She's the most prominent arts patron and political contributor in town. I don't know her, but I'd definitely see if I can find someone to introduce you to her."

Make a wish list of people you would like to add to your power circles for the purpose of achieving your goals. These can be specific individuals ("David Parker, top institutional investor for XYZ Bank") or categories ("someone high up in the office of the secretary of labor"). The key question is, "Whom do I need, and how do I reach them?" You can start with groups like the Chamber of Commerce, Rotary, and Kiwanis, because through them you'll meet many people who can help you identify the people you need to know.

Don't be afraid to think big *and* small. There's no reason you can't reach those at the top of their industries or professions, and there's no reason you should ignore those who can provide you with an easy entry to a particular ecosystem at a lower level.

Your wish list goal is twofold. First, you want to fill any holes you may have in your current power circles when it comes to the eight key ecosystems. Most of us have a good number of connections in friends and family, career or profession, and passions and interests, but how are you in the finance, government and politics, media, industry, and community systems? Second, make sure you have enough connections, with enough influence, in each ecosystem. You may know three bankers, for example, but if they're all at the local level and can access loan amounts only up to $1 million, what will you do if you need a business loan for more than that?

Goals are valuable because they force us to think about future needs. In the same way, you must think about your power circles not in terms of what they provide you currently but in terms of what you will need in the future—and the connections you must add to get there.

Step 11: Make a plan to reach out to new connections during the next three to six months.

Adding new connections starts with asking your current power circle members what they can do to help. They may begin by educating you about a particular ecosystem. I talk with a lot of entrepreneurs who are seeking funding but who don't really know the first thing about venture capital. I give them several books and articles to read and a few industry blogs to check out, and I say, "Let's talk in two weeks when you've had a chance to absorb the basics." Once you know the fundamentals, you can ask people in your power circles the key question: "Who do you think I need to know in order to do X? And can you introduce me?"

Being introduced by people who already have credibility in a particular ecosystem will help you be taken seriously. It's essentially "borrowing" their credibility in order to open the door. That credibility should be considered a sacred trust. When your power circle members introduce you to people in their networks, they are essentially endowing you with some of their social capital. If you mess up, it will reflect badly on them. You must honor the introduction by being a person of integrity and doing your best to add value to your connections' connections.

Remember, however, getting to the right connection is rarely a straight line. It's more like a matrix, a web of connections, or overlapping circles of the networks of the networks of your connections. If you want to reach Warren Buffett, for instance, one of your business associates may know someone in Omaha whose mother knows a woman whose husband plays bridge at the same club as Buffett. Or your son may go to school with the grandson of a vice president at Berkshire Hathaway. Put the request out to your network, and you'll be amazed at the paths you will follow to get where you want to go.

If your power circles don't have connections in the ecosystems you are targeting, do some research. Check Twitter and LinkedIn; see which bloggers, writers, and publications cover this area. Which names crop up regularly in this particular field? Which companies and organizations are important, who are their key players, and how can you reach them? Remember, entrance into an ecosystem can be gained by going up, down, or sideways. Getting access to the governor might be difficult, but reaching out to the governor's political advisor or head of his local fund-raising efforts might be much easier. And it could be that the access you truly need isn't at the top, but rather, it will come from people on the "front lines," so to speak. If you want to launch an educational product targeted toward the college market, for example, eventually you may need access to university bookstores and social media sites like Twitter. But to start with, wouldn't it be more important to gain access to the college students themselves to do your market research? In that case, your daughter's friends in the local chapter of her sorority might be exactly the people you need to reach.

Remember that one of the easiest ways to enter many ecosystems is by joining key groups within it. Many industries have professional associations; communities have different interest groups that support things like community planning for safer neighborhoods, after-school programs, and so on. Political and financial ecosystems will often intersect with the charitable, religious, or sports ecosystems in your city. However, you want to be smart about the groups you join. Many people in the local Chamber of Commerce or Kiwanis Club are there just to promote their particular business or service.

There's nothing wrong with that, of course—but perhaps more of your time would be better spent with more powerful groups where you may meet not only people at your level and those just getting started but also some of the more influential individuals in your community.

As the quality of the groups you join goes up, so does the quality of the opportunities provided. Often one of your power circle members may clue you in to a particular group where movers and shakers congregate. In 2011 my good friend Jackie Zehner mentioned a group called Alley to the Valley, a network of "the world's most influential women in venture, entrepreneurship, business, politics, and media." It was at an Alley to the Valley summit where I met Barbara Corcoran (business expert, real estate mogul, and one of the "shark" investors on the *Shark Tank* TV show), among dozens of other powerhouses. Whatever your industry or business, there are groups and associations of powerful people within it. You need to know these organizations so you can (1) join them, (2) show up at their meetings, and (3) add value to their members and the organizations to the best of your ability.

Finding the proper connections in each ecosystem is critical, of course, but you need to be selective about the connections you choose to add to your power circles. As you reach out to new people, ask yourself, "Do they match my values? What will they add to my network? Will they bring diversity to my power circles, or is this yet another connection of the same kind? Is this person opening up a new ecosystem for me? Am I connecting both up, down, and sideways? Is this someone I admire and can learn from, or can this person perhaps learn from me? Do I want to emulate this person's core behaviors and professional attributes?" Remember, adding one bad apple to your network can damage your reputation and social capital with the entire group. Be very careful whom you include in your power circles because your connections are the most important assets you possess. You want to make sure you are building power circles filled with meaningful relationships that are beneficial to all parties, where values are shared and each individual is willing to contribute to the others' success.

7

Phase 2: Target, Connect, and Engage—Maximize Your Time with Every Connection

....

I don't have a Rolodex. I have relationships.

—DAVID BAKER, AVALON INTERNATIONAL GROUP

Power connectors are very deliberate in seeking out the people and ecosystems to add to their Key 50 and Vital 100; but they also are open to the magic of synchronistic meetings. Recently I met Dr. Reatha Clark King while we were both brushing our teeth in the ladies' room at Reagan National Airport near Washington, DC. I discovered she was the former head of the General Mills Foundation and now chairs the National Association of Corporate Directors. Since then we have spoken frequently about corporate boards, and she has given me wonderful advice and guidance. This meeting was yet another proof that every person you connect with—in person, or through e-mail, phone, LinkedIn, or Facebook—may become an important friend, ally, mentor, or colleague, so you must be prepared to maximize your interactions with anyone you meet.

In Phase 2 of power connecting, you must *target*, *connect*, and *engage*. You must identify the people (or the kinds of people) you wish to meet and the best places to meet them. Then you must develop the skills to create a connection with them in three minutes or less. Finally, you have to engage them by adding enough value and developing enough intrigue to ensure that you will be more than just another business card, introduction, or encounter.

There's a French term, *bricolage*, which means "tinkering," or making do with whatever comes to hand. I think of it as being scrappy and resourceful. There never is a perfect time for a connection, so you must make it happen. Think strategically: Given that I have A and B but lack C and have no money, how do I gain access to C? There is always a way around it, over it, under it, or through it, and the path inevitably is created by your connections. This phase is critical in finding the connections you need, reaching out to them effectively, and then taking the first steps that will lay the foundation to solid future relationships.

Step 1: Target and Be Ready

> There are people you need to know. I may not always know
> how they will help you, or what ultimately will come of
> the introductions—but I know, and you know, that these
> relationships will be important to you in some way.
> **—JAY ALLEN, PRESIDENT AND COFOUNDER, CXO**

In Chapter 6 you identified the ecosystems, and certain individuals within them, that you believe will help you reach your goals. You created a plan for reaching out to those people through your power circles, associations, key individuals in that ecosystem, and so on. Now you need to discover as much as possible about their interests, professional credentials, hobbies and charities, association memberships, marital status, and number of children—anything that will help you build a connection and, eventually, a relationship.

Depending on the individual, sites like LinkedIn and Facebook, as well as corporate and association biographies, will give you basic information. Your power circles also may be able to add more details. Even if they don't know someone personally, their networks may have some connection or at least some knowledge about those you want to reach. However, before you actually meet these people, you must answer three essential questions: Who are you? What are you ready to give? And what are you looking for? You must develop what I call your *share*, your *value-add*, and your *ask*.

Your Share

As Susan Cain points out, business is based on a culture of extroversion: "To advance our careers, we're expected to promote ourselves unabashedly."[1] You say hello and start a conversation, but as soon as someone asks, "What do you do?" it's as if a switch is flipped and you launch into 30 seconds of polished, practiced, extroverted, self-congratulatory self-promotion—the "elevator speech." Well, I for one detest elevator speeches—since when did 30 seconds of self-promotion create any kind of genuine, person-to-person connection? I believe that you need to give people a sense of who you *are* before you tell them what you do, and that's what your share is designed to do. It is a way of telling your story that educates others about your heart, head, and gut. It helps people know you and (hopefully) begin to like you, so that trusting you will follow.

Your share should include who you are, what you're about, and what you're interested in. Start with personal details; talk about your family, your hobbies, and your civic or community involvements. I have a good friend who begins his introduction by talking about how he loves to ride horses and that his favorite relaxation is taking kids on hikes near his home so they can watch hawks and eagles flying overhead. Your personal story doesn't have to make a "splash," but it should give people a sense of who you are in life.

Next, include a few sentences about your business or profession that reflect your energy and passion about what you do. Think of ways to make your description interesting and intriguing, even provocative. For example, a venture capitalist might say, "I do my darnedest to say yes to people when they're looking for money for their businesses. Let me tell you about the craziest business we ever funded." Or an entrepreneur might mention, "Five colleagues and I are developing an Internet-based program to train 10,000 new midwives in India. Did you know that in 2011 more than 309,000 infants in India died the same day they were born?" Remember, this is not a promotion of what you do but a story that demonstrates your passion and energy for your business or profession.

Your share is a chance to educate others on exactly who you are. But remember, it's a declaration you will need to live up to, so it had better be authentic. "The currency of the Relationship Era ... is not awareness, nor even quality; it is authenticity," wrote Bob Garfield and Doug Levy in *Can't Buy Me Like: How Authentic Customer Connections Drive Superior Results*.[2]

I suggest that you outline your share and become familiar with the main points you want to include from your personal and professional lives, but don't turn it into a rehearsed "speech." If you are not comfortable doing this kind of thing (and I know many people aren't), keep it short, and speak from the heart. Imagine a good friend you haven't seen for years has asked you to tell her what you're up to these days. How nervous would you be to share what you were excited and passionate about in your life? And if you're still nervous when you're asked to talk about yourself, be honest about that. "Be yourself, and people will respond to your honesty," says Aassia Haq, chief marketing officer (CMO) of MBO Partners, a leading provider of independent consultant engagement and compliance solutions. Just let your share reflect who you are at your best.

Your Value-Add

Your story opens the door to a relationship, but the value you add will solidify it. If you want people to reach out to you and include you in their network, they'll do so faster if you have something to offer—and if you give it before you ask for something in return. As Jay Allen, president and cofounder of CXO, a private networking group for executives, writes, "I know that I must earn the right to build a relationship with you. I know that in order to earn that right, I have to provide something of value. I am making the decision to provide that value and pursue a relationship regardless of the outcome of any ultimate benefit to myself."[3]

If you are just starting out, or if you are approaching someone with a lot more clout and position, you may wonder what value you can provide. But I've found that everyone has a unique set of experiences and connections that might solve others' problems or augment their gifts. Look at your lists of accomplishments, strengths, and connections, all of which represent value you can provide to others. Your value can be your knowledge, or your network, or even just your ability to listen and empathize. An outside perspective and willingness to tell the truth also can be of significant value.

I was invited to meet with some of the top people in an organization that provides funding for entrepreneurial women. Very quickly I could see that there were some problems with their current strategies, and I decided that I needed to speak up. "The way you've been doing things doesn't take crowdfunding into account." I offered several suggestions, and afterward the hostess (a billionaire in her own right) asked for my business card and called me the next day to discuss the matter in greater depth.

If you doubt your ability to add value, keep these questions in mind: "How can I help?" and "Can any of my contacts be of assistance?" Simply asking those questions will ensure that you enter any relationship with a focus on what you can give to others.

Your Ask

For people to help you, they need to know what you are doing and what you need. That's where your ask comes in. This is not a direct request— "Can you fund my start-up?"—but a clear delineation of your endeavors and whatever assistance would be of benefit, no matter who or where it comes from. Here's an example: "I own a training company that specializes in cross-cultural customer service. We have offices in Chicago and Dubai, and we're looking for partners to help us expand into Asia."

I believe there are three reasons that it's critical to determine your ask in advance. First, your ask needs to match the ecosystem and "room" you're in as well as the person you're meeting. For instance, I frequently see people approach high-tech VCs asking for money to fund a business that has nothing to do with technology—it's the right ecosystem (finance) but the wrong room. Or perhaps someone owns a manufacturing business that he's looking to expand overseas, but he asks his buddies at the local softball game if they know of any experts on China. His buddies might lead to the right individual eventually, but why not do your research to find the right room and then make sure your request is appropriate for the people you're asking? I usually suggest to people that when they are crafting their ask, they should make sure that it fits with the ecosystems they need to enter. The manufacturer who wants to expand into China and needs information from the political and industry ecosystems might say, "I'm looking for someone who has experience with the regulatory environment for manufacturing widgets in China."

Second, you need to make sure that your ask is appropriate for the stage of the relationship. When most people first start dating as teenagers, they will rehearse over and over exactly how they're going to ask someone out, what they'll say and how they'll act on the date, and what to do when it comes time to say goodnight. And the smart people know that if they ask for too much on that first date, they run the risk of having doors slammed in their faces. It's the same in a business relationship. You can't try to go from point A to point Z in one meeting without the risk of having the door slammed on you. Nevertheless, I've seen people go up to someone at a conference and say, "I need $1 million to get my business going." Well, nobody's going to give a stranger $1 million. This kind of inappropriate ask damages credibility and delays the "know you, like you, trust you" sequence so essential to connection. Inappropriate asks indicate that you haven't done your research, and you will be labeled an amateur. Your ask must be appropriate to the closeness of the relationship at that particular moment.

Third, coming up with your ask in advance will allow you to eliminate any fear you may have about asking for help. In *The Generosity Network*, fundraiser Jennifer McCrea and philanthropist Jeff Walker list five "terrors" associated with asking for money: societal taboos associated with its discussion, fear of rejection, being seen as a "salesperson," putting yourself in the position of a suppliant, and embarrassment about being in need.[4] However, asking for any kind of help can bring up the same emotions. Remember that your ask is actually opening the door to a new relationship from which both parties can benefit. Crafting the ask in advance, tailoring it for the right ecosystem, the right room, and the right level of relationship, and rehearsing it until you're comfortable—all of these will help reduce your fear and make your ask more natural.

Through years of doing a *lot* of asking, as well as helping others to ask appropriately, I've come up with the six secrets of a great ask.

1. *Start small.* Once granted, a small request opens the door to other requests and favors. Influence expert Dr. Robert Cialdini calls this *commitment* and *consistency.* Once we've made a commitment to someone, we tend to want to stay consistent with our decision and therefore will grant more requests. Your first ask might be for a moment of a person's time, or a short meeting, or a referral. Small, easily satisfied requests allow you to build the relationship one step at a time.

Often the best thing to ask for first is advice. It puts the giver in a position of knowledge and power, and the receiver may learn something or gain a new and valuable perspective. Studies show that those who seek advice from others at work are regarded more favorably than colleagues who don't.[5] An easy way to phrase the request might be, "If you were in my shoes, what would you do?"

2. ***Make your ask specific***. Saying to a PR expert, "I need to get on TV—can you help me?" is not specific. "The YMCA is starting its fall campaign in eight weeks, and we have a big-name basketball star scheduled to headline our first event; who do you know at the local TV stations that I could contact with the story?" is a clear, direct, specific ask, and it is much easier to fulfill.

3. ***Make your ask appropriate to the person, room, and ecosystem.*** The appropriateness of your ask makes it clear you've done your research and you know what people can and cannot provide.

4. ***Build your ask around a story that expresses your passion.*** People buy with emotion and justify with logic, and the same is true when it comes to "selling" your ask. Instead of laying out your needs logically, tell a story that will engage both you and your listener. Take the example of the YMCA campaign above. You could phrase your ask like this: "Every night 200 kids in our downtown area hang out on the streets because they have nowhere to go. Some of them are homeless, some come from broken homes; they're ripe pickings for the gangs and other predators. The YMCA has been trying for 10 years to build a facility downtown so these kids will have a place to play basketball and other sports, swim, hang out, take classes, and learn to do something with their lives. As part of our campaign to raise the final $10 million, the starting center of the city's NBA team is coming to the groundbreaking next month, and he's going to shoot hoops with some of the kids. Who do you know at the local TV stations that I could contact to get some coverage?" As former movie mogul Peter Guber once said, "Aim for the heart, not the wallet." Your story is the heart of your ask.

5. ***Be willing to ask for help.*** "Help" is not a word many people use easily. We are taught that we should be self-sufficient and make our own way. However, I've found that using the words "Please help me" will get people moving. I spoke on an entrepreneur's panel in 2013, and I asked for a copy of the video of my speech. After no response to three or four e-mails, I finally wrote,

"Please help me get this done." Not only did I get an immediate response, but the conference organizer also offered to film a professional introduction to add to the video.

6. *Whether or not people are able to fulfill your ask, express your gratitude for their time and ask them to keep you in mind.* Even if you have the right room, the right ecosystem, and the right people, it might not be the right time or conditions for your particular ask. Thank them for hearing you out, and then say, "Keep me in mind." If you've been clear on your share, and if you've demonstrated that you have value to add, even if they can't help you themselves, they may be the conduit to someone who can fill your need.

Once you choose the people whom you wish to reach, and you prepare your share, value-add, and ask, you must figure out how to get in touch. Should you e-mail or phone them? Send a request through LinkedIn? Go to their office? Approach them at a conference or other professional occasion? All are appropriate depending on the individual and your particular circumstances, but the best way to connect with anyone is with a personal introduction from a mutual connection. A personal introduction allows you to borrow credibility from someone who already has it. It also will give you and the other person something in common immediately; you can both talk about your relationship to "John Smith." Even if the connection is a weak link (that is, someone your connection knows only distantly), being able to use his or her name will open many doors, start your meeting on a slightly warmer note, and help you establish rapport quickly.

Step 2: Meet and Immediately Connect

> If you want to form meaningful bonds that lead to
> productive collaboration and innovation,
> make room for more close encounters.
> —KEITH FERRAZZI

Whether it is a face-to-face meeting, over the phone, or online, you have only a short window of time either to create a strong connection or to become another forgotten face in the crowd. If you wish to create a lasting impression no matter how brief the encounter, follow these guidelines drawn from observing master connectors in every industry. (Many of these refer to in-person meetings, but they can easily be applied to phone or online contacts.) Some of these suggestions may seem intuitive, but you must ask yourself how many you actually implement *every* time you meet someone new.

Your personal style speaks long before you open your mouth. Make what you say and how you look suitable. Most people can recognize quality clothing and jewelry, and they will notice yours. Dress appropriately for the situation, meeting place, and goal of the meeting. If you're clueless about style, a good department store, women's boutique, or men's store will often have people who can help you choose outfits. Buy the best quality you can afford. (And notice other people's clothing. I have found that complimenting women and men on a jacket, a tie, or a piece of jewelry is an excellent way to open a conversation, and vice versa—wearing something unique yourself can be an ice-breaker for others.) On the phone or in an online contact, make sure your speaking and writing styles are professional and appropriate. Watch your grammar and spelling, please—mistakes make you look sloppy and uneducated.

Look approachable. We've all seen people walking down a hall or in the corner of a room, their postures and facial expressions making it very clear they're not open to conversation. Nowadays, it's much more likely to see people with their heads down and their attention fixed on smartphone screens. (According to one study, most smartphone users check their phones every six and a half minutes.[6]) If you want to connect, take your eyes off of your phone and get interested in the people around you.

Say hello. Statistics show only 2 percent of our conversations are with strangers.[7] That means that many of us pass like ships in the night, not realizing what we have missed by not offering a kind word or a smile to a stranger. The transition from stranger to acquaintance can take less than five seconds if you're willing to be the first to break the ice. You may have heard about the Marriott "15/5 rule": whenever an employee comes within 15 feet of anyone in a Marriott hotel, the employee acknowledges the guest with eye contact or a friendly nod. If the guest comes within 5 feet, the employee smiles and says hello. Take on the Marriott rule for yourself, and be the first to reach out.

The first three minutes of a connection are vital for building rapport. You have only a brief time to make a strong first impression, so maximize those first three minutes. Give a firm handshake. Smile—as Goldie Hawn once said, "I have witnessed the softening of the hardest of hearts by a simple smile." Say the other person's name. Start a conversation by asking a question. Offer a sincere compliment if appropriate. Be attentive to body language and tone of voice. Think of this person as if he or she were going to become one of your best friends, and then do your best to discover what you like about him or her.

Be fully present and listen. Ever had someone's attention wander while you were talking? Research by the Associated Press states that the average attention span in 2012 was a whopping 8 seconds, down from 12 seconds in 2000.[8] In contrast, the best communicators excel at putting their full attention on others. Bill Clinton is known for his ability to be fully present even when he is with someone for a few seconds or less. Give the people you are meeting the courtesy of your full attention when you are with them. It will make you more memorable and your communication richer.

I've also found that the more you listen, the stronger the connection others will feel with you. According to a 2012 study, good listening skills are tied to better parenting, marital relationships, sales performance, and customer service satisfaction. Furthermore, good listeners are more liked, rated as more attractive, garner more trust, and are more likely to produce greater academic achievement and upward mobility in the workplace.[9] Pretend this stranger is a close friend, or try focusing on him or her as if you couldn't see and could only listen. McCrea and Walker suggest what they call the SIM test. At the end of any conversation ask, "What surprised me? What inspired me? What moved me?" If you can't answer at least one, you probably weren't listening.[10]

Ask great questions. Sherwood Neiss of Crowdfund Capital Advisors says, "I love to ask questions, and I love people who love to ask questions. I think every encounter should be the game 21 questions!" If you ask people questions about themselves, their businesses, their families, and their interests, you make them feel important. And when you listen to their answers with your eyes, ears, and heart, you will learn and understand more about them than you can imagine. Combining the ability to ask great questions with the skill of listening fully to the answers will help you turn even the briefest connection into a memorable encounter.

These basics of connecting happen in the first three minutes, before you ever launch into your share, your value-add, or your ask. Indeed, at this point you've probably said very little about yourself, especially if you've been asking questions and listening. But if you want to create the foundation for a real relationship, you must deepen your rapport and set the stage for a longer-term connection. You need what I call the *skills of engagement.*

Step 3: Engage—Deepen the Connection and Set the Stage for More

> I believe that every time people talk together in a social and mutually gratifying way, the world becomes a better place.
> —DANIEL MENAKER, *A GOOD TALK*

When Anu Bharwadj was pursuing her MBA at the Stockholm School of Economics, she was invited to a private dinner at the residence of the dean, and she was seated next to Par Jorgen Parsson, the founder and partner of North-Zone Ventures, a prominent technology investment partnership in Europe. "At the time, I was in the process of starting a nonprofit foundation that was focused on global entrepreneurship," Anu remembers. "As a result of the relationship that grew from one dinner conversation, NorthZone became one of our anchor sponsors. Then, when I started a company focused on helping private equity and venture capital funds access capital in various parts of Asia, the Middle East, and the Nordics, NorthZone was one of my first clients."

Your goal in power connecting is to be able to turn even a simple dinner conversation into a lasting strategic relationship. In this step you are starting to explore each other's values, seeing what you have in common and the potential for mutual benefit and regard. If you approach this step with curiosity and the intent to provide value, it can be extremely enjoyable for both you and the other party.

The following are the keys to successful engagement.

Find something in common: a person, location, experience, or point of view. When marketing and branding consultant Dorie Clark interviewed Robert Cialdini, he gave her some excellent advice: The way to get someone to like you immediately is to find a commonality. Almost any commonality, no matter how trivial—a shared alma mater, an interest in running, a love of dogs—will get the ball rolling. Common ground gives you a place from which to build the foundation of a relationship. The place you're meeting, the person who introduced you, a profession, the kind of cocktail you like—finding something in common creates a degree of similarity between you and the other person, and it inevitably makes you more likable. I can strike up great conversations with people on airplanes or in airports simply because we're both in transit.

Your share can come into play the instant you find something in common. This is a great chance to talk about what you're passionate about while still keeping the focus on the other person. Share a little about your common experience, ask the other person a question, and then let him or her talk. You will find out much more and create a much stronger relationship if you share a little and listen a lot about your commonalities.

Even if you feel you have nothing in common with someone—maybe you're just getting started in business and the connection you'd like to make is with the most successful entrepreneur in your field—you can be sure that somewhere along the line you will have at least one experience in common, and that's the human experience. Anyone who's started a business will have gone through similar ups and downs, exhilarations and efforts. Find a way to relate your passion to the other person's, and you'll automatically feel more in tune. But even if you have little in common, don't worry. Some of the value you may be able to provide will come from the differences of perspective and experience you can bring to the relationship.

Find out who they are—discover what is important to them professionally and, more important, personally. When I was working on a deal recently, I met an attorney from Boston. As we were talking, he mentioned that his dog had died not long before, and it was clear how much the dog had meant to him. A couple of months later I found a lovely YouTube video of a dog and a baby and I sent it to him, indicating I had thought of him and the loss of his pet. When I saw him and his wife at a function three months later, I inquired if they were thinking of getting a new dog, and they both were surprised that I remembered. These kinds of multiple "touches" on personal interest demonstrate that you are listening intently for and care about what is most important to the other person.

I believe that all individuals are unique, and it's my job to discover what makes them so. On the professional side, I want to find out about their career or business, what sets them apart, where they see themselves in the next few years, what they have to offer (it might be of benefit to my power circles), and what kinds of advice and help they might need. Understanding their professional world will allow me to make appropriate recommendations for them. For example, I met a scientist who had been trying to get funding for a medical device from her local network. After speaking with her, it was clear that she was asking the wrong people, at the wrong level, in the wrong location, for help. I was able to put her in touch with a different set of investors who specialize in the medical industry and who were in line with the scientist's goals of creating wealth while doing good.

Bob Burg is the well-known author of *Endless Referrals* and *The Go-Giver*, and he knows quite a lot about connecting with others. "The best way to provide value for others is to focus on them and find out about them by asking questions they enjoy answering—like, 'How did you get started in business?' If you ask about what they do and what they enjoy most, and you actively listen, you'll find it easy to create a relationship."

Whenever you get to know what's vital to people personally, it creates a deeper connection. Financier and philanthropist Michael Milken once said that everyone is trying to be successful, loved, and healthy, and that's why the three things that are important to most people are their money, their children, and their health. When you understand what people are passionate about and/or proud of in their careers, their families, and their lives, you open the door to the potential for lasting connection.

If someone isn't a good fit, smile and move on. When you've gotten to know people and you've learned what's important to them, it should be evident fairly quickly if they are a solid fit with you—meaning that your values and behaviors are compatible. But sometimes you discover that the match just isn't right. They may not like you or your style; you may not be in tune with their goals or their beliefs about life and other people. Or perhaps you get the sense that these people are what Wharton professor Adam Grant, an expert on giving and the author of *Give and Take*, terms "takers," people who put themselves and their needs before anyone else's.

If the connection isn't right, feel free to smile and move on. No one, including you, is going to be a good match for every single human being they meet. You don't want everyone in your power circles, or even numbered among your acquaintances. However, even if someone is not a match for you, you can still be helpful with advice, judicious referrals, and so on. Your goal is for "nonmatches" to part from you with a positive experience.

Share and be real. For people to open up about themselves, you need to open up too. You must be willing to talk about what's important to you, and to do so genuinely. That's not usually what we do in business relationships— but creating connection is hard without it. Dorie Clark remarks, "We all have our 'professional aura' around us, but the sooner you can develop a real connection, talking about real things, the better. Taking off the veneer and talking about your hopes, your goals, and your struggles is one way to connect deeply and quickly."

Being real means acknowledging your flaws and challenges and being open about your passions. It means not having to express yourself perfectly in the conversation, being human rather than robotic, letting your enthusiasm come through even when it's not "cool" to do so (have you ever talked on and on about your favorite sports team?), and being willing to share your feelings as well as who or what you know. And hopefully, being real will allow others to be equally real with you.

Put yourself in other people's shoes. What would they want and value? What help might they need? When you find out what's most important to people, and you share with them genuinely, it naturally produces feelings of empathy. But empathy is only the first step; for creating connections, you must use your feelings of empathy and "other-based" perspective to determine what the other person wants, values, and needs.

When a friend of mine was four years old, his mother said to him, "Dave, your father's birthday is coming up. What do you think Daddy would like to have?" Dave thought about it, then replied, "I think Daddy would like a scooter." From that time forward, a "scooter" was the family name for a gift you give to someone else when you really want it yourself. I think when it comes to providing value and offering help, sometimes our tendency is to give what we would like in the same circumstances rather than what the other person really needs. When I look back on the times when I've felt uneasy about helping someone, it was usually because I was thinking more of myself than the other person. Get out of your own way, put yourself into the other person's shoes, and listen intently for what that person wants and needs. Sometimes the simplest way to do this is to ask, "How can I help?" Even if the answer is, "Nothing," most people will appreciate—and remember—the offer.

Give or add value immediately. Power connectors are experts at adding value immediately to anyone they meet (value defined by what the other person wants and needs). Giving first is rare, and it builds trust in a world where talk is cheap and people mistrustful. In the Jewish community, this attitude of always adding value is called "being a mensch." Mensches help people who cannot help them; they help as many people as they can, and they help without the expectation of return. Luckily, there are so many different ways to create value—a contact, an introduction, an insight, advice, a favor, potential business—as long as it links directly to the person's personal and professional interests.

One of my favorite value-adds is information. (There's a fascinating study showing that whenever we encounter new information, the brain automatically starts thinking about who else might be interested in it.[11]) I'll mention a book or article I've read or direct someone to a website that has some important statistics or data. I also love to refer people to experts I've used in the past. This provides them with information and potential assistance, and it also creates a possible connection with people in my power circles.

Think of value-adds as anything that can (1) save time, (2) save money, (3) save someone's sanity, (4) eliminate stress, or (5) bring more fun to someone's life. In some circumstances, providing a sympathetic ear or being a sounding board for someone's ideas can add great value in the moment. Telling the truth when others won't can provide great value, as can challenging people to get out of their own way and do something about their situation. And at times a simple acknowledgment or a "thank you" can add the right value at the right moment.

The best kinds of value-adds create greater opportunity and serve others at a higher level. iParenting Media and 30Second Mobile founder Elisa All was the recipient of just such a value-add at the beginning of her career: "I am grateful for my boss at the television station where I worked after I graduated college. He gave me the opportunity to work in media for the first time, and that triggered my desire to go back for my master's degree in journalism at Northwestern University. Despite the fact that he didn't want me to leave my position at the station, he wrote me an excellent letter of recommendation, which I'm sure helped me along my journey. A master's in journalism from Northwestern built the foundation I needed to have a successful career as a media entrepreneur." I believe the greatest value you can give is to open doors for others and help them be and do more in their lives.

Mention your ask, but don't "sell" it. Only *after* you've added value should you talk about your own needs and wants. Think of this as a "tease" rather than a request. You want them to know something about you and your business and what you are working on at the moment so they can keep you in mind. Remember, relationships actually grow stronger if both parties have the chance to give and receive. You are giving people information that will allow them to offer help to you at some point down the line. Mentioning your ask helps to lay the foundation for a professional relationship between two equal partners.

Create intrigue—lay the foundation for another meeting. Many people make the mistake of trying to impress a potential connection in this first meeting. But to develop a long-term relationship, your goal is not to impress but to create intrigue. Communication expert Robert Dilenschneider calls this the "deep bump": you make contact quickly, establish enough of a connection to secure the next meeting, and then move on.

Presentation experts say that whenever you give a speech, you should ask yourself, "What's the one critical piece of information I want to leave with the audience?" Try asking yourself something similar here: "What's the one thing I can say that will lay a foundation for a future connection?" A few years ago I attended a private conference in New York where the prominent angel investor and philanthropist Esther Dyson was speaking. I'd admired Esther for a long time and wanted to talk with her, but at the end of the conference there was a long line of people waiting to catch her ear. Because I had done my research, I knew that Esther specialized in energy investing. So when I got to the front of the line, I said hello, mentioned a couple of energy deals that I knew about, told her I admired her passion for investing, gave her my card, and said, "It's a pleasure to speak with you." Three sentences and I was done. That night I had a LinkedIn invitation from Esther with a request to stay in touch.

As Martin Zwilling comments, "Great connectors don't just fall into conversations. They carefully shape them with conscious intent and tone."[12] Once you've discovered what someone really wants and needs and you've added value in those areas, you've done what's necessary to lay the foundation for future contact. As they say in show business, get off the stage and leave 'em wanting more.

Capture their data, and make a commitment to follow up quickly. For you to be able to stay in contact, however, you need to capture their data efficiently and elegantly in the moment. Get and give a business card (if they have one—many people just connect on LinkedIn over their smartphones right then and there). Make sure your card lists multiple ways to reach you: phone, e-mail, LinkedIn contact information, website, and so on. If appropriate, before I give my own card, I might say, "Wait a moment, let me give you my direct number," and then I'll handwrite the number on the back. In many Asian countries, you must carefully look at someone's card before you put it away; to do otherwise is considered rude. However, the practice of actually looking at a card in the moment is a wise step because you can see exactly what information it provides, and what it does not.

Depending on the individual, I might ask, "What's the best way to reach you?" or "What's the name of your assistant?" and then I'll make a note on the card. No matter how you capture information—on your phone, in Outlook, in the "Relationship" section of the other person's LinkedIn profile—make a note of where and when you met this person and any details that might be helpful in the future. Coming back from a meeting with nothing but a business card and a vague memory of someone's details will not help you build strong strategic relationships. Power connecting requires systems, not memory. In the next chapter you'll learn how to incorporate new information and new connections into your power circles.

As you prepare to leave, make a commitment to follow up with them soon—and do so. If you've created enough intrigue, your offer will be welcome. But before you go . . .

Ask Three Golden Questions. I often teach people Buckminster Fuller's "corridor principle." Imagine looking down a corridor with a long row of doors on either side, but all the doors are shut. Inevitably the door you think will open won't—but the one next to it will. In business relationships, most people stop after one connection when the person they really need is three links away. Before you leave any meeting or encounter, you always should ask what I call the Three Golden Questions.

First, *"How can I help you?"* This gives you an opportunity to add value immediately with a suggestion, a referral, or an opportunity, and it will establish you as a giver and potentially someone they want to know.

Second, *"What ideas do you have for me?"* Asking for ideas allows the people you are talking with to add value to you as you have (hopefully) added value to them.

Third, *"Who else do you know that I should talk to?"* The very connection you need may be in this individual's network, and the only way you can find out is with this question.

Once you ask these questions, be quiet and listen. If you've engaged the other person throughout your conversation, you may be delighted at the answers you receive. Then conclude your conversation with a simple yet powerful statement: "Happy to help." The other person will likely remember it when you contact him or her again.

Not every conversation will lead to a new addition to your power circles. Not every favor you do or piece of valuable information you pass along will be returned. Sometimes you may just have a friendly talk, wish him or her a wonderful life, and never meet again. Whether or not your conversations and meetings turn into lasting relationships, I believe that being fully present and offering value to someone is the rent we pay for our time on earth. I also believe that in every meeting you can learn something new, gain a new experience, and perhaps find a new friend or associate. The more you offer, the more people you connect with, the more opportunities and relationships will come your way.

8

Phase 3: Reconnect, Assess and Activate, and Multiply Value

The ability to get things done with collaborative networks
is the next evolution in human productivity.

—MICHAEL LEAVITT AND RICH MCKEOWN,
FINDING ALLIES, BUILDING ALLIANCES

After you've met, connected, and engaged with someone (either in person, on the phone, or online), the real relationship building can begin. Phase 3 of power connecting is integrating new people into your network with a three-step process: (1) immediately reconnect; (2) assess the connection and activate your system; and (3) multiply value and deepen the relationship.

Recently one of my power circle members introduced me to a woman who is a high-powered consultant at Accenture. She came to the United States from South Korea and needed help in learning how to build connections. I met with her, and on the drive home I sent her a text message (Step 1) telling her I had already made a phone call to one person on her behalf and would follow up with her again within 24 hours. At home I sent a LinkedIn request and provided e-mail introductions to other people who are in my power circles. (This is called *triangulation*, which you'll learn about in Chapter 9.) She replied immediately—a very good sign for Step 2, assessing this contact and seeing if he or she is suitable for my power circles. (Often I will reconnect, add as much value as I can, and then see what the reaction is. Some people don't respond, effectively "opting out" of my network. This woman opted in by quickly thanking me and offering to help me in any way she could.)

I did a more little research on her (Step 2), and I found out that she had been very poor growing up in Korea. Her parents couldn't even afford to buy her a piece of gum, so she used to look for wads of gum on the street, dust them off, and then chew them. She had risen from these very humble beginnings to a very successful business career. *Wow,* I thought, *this is a woman I want to know,* so I added her to my Vital 100. I reached out again to discover a little more about her goals so that I could multiply value and deepen the relationship (Step 3). She told me she had been thinking about writing a book and possibly developing a speaking career. I connected her with my literary agent, sent her a copy of my book proposal, and told her I would put her in touch with all of the people who had been helping me with press and PR for this book.

This entire process took perhaps 45 minutes, yet we both had gained a great new connection and the potential to benefit from each other's networks. That's the great thing about being a power connector: with every new contact, you have the opportunity to increase your connections not just by one, but by multiples of 10 to 100—as long as you choose wisely, follow up well, and then put in the effort needed to stay connected.

The first step in this phase is to reach out and reconnect with those you meet, whether it's in person or through e-mail, social media, or phone.

Step 1: Reconnect Immediately

> It's totally pointless to amass a pile of business cards that you
> do nothing with. Follow up right after meeting people,
> and try to get on their calendar again ASAP.
> —ERIN VALENTI, TECHNOLOGY ENTREPRENEUR

Toya Powell, director of government engagement for the U.S. Black Chamber, once said, "Fortune is in the follow-up." How many people do you meet in a given year? And how many of them follow up within 24 hours of meeting you, even with all the different means we have of instantaneous communication?

Even though it seems that we're expected to be available 24/7, the number of people who actually respond quickly to communication requests is very small. Internet marketing specialist Neil Patel declares that your communication shows how much you care and if you are on top of things. He says, "Responding within 24 hours at the latest is a requirement."[1] Simply reaching out to others quickly will set you apart.

Coming back from meetings, introductions, conferences, phone calls, or e-mails in which you have maximized your encounters with other people, you need to reconnect immediately—meaning, a personalized e-mail or LinkedIn request within 24 hours. Thank them for the meeting, invite them to stay connected with you, and then include something that you believe will be of value to them. Your e-mail could include an article or link to a resource online, a suggestion for someone to contact and/or an introduction, or information about an upcoming opportunity. You also should check their contact information to ensure that you have their complete details, and if not, you should include a request for any missing pieces. Finally, tell them what you are working on so they will know how they might help you. Here's a sample follow-up e-mail or LinkedIn request:

To: Sam Smith
From: Judy Robinett
Re: Great to meet you yesterday!

Dear Sam—Thanks for a stimulating conversation in the airport. I agree with you that the future of technology is going to be in the ways it makes it easier for us to connect, communicate, and collaborate.

Attached is the article I mentioned yesterday about Peter Mason— his algorithms around networking are completely cutting edge, and he's definitely someone you should know. I'd be happy to set up an introduction on LinkedIn for you. (I sent you a LinkedIn request earlier today. Also, do you have a Twitter account? If so, can you let me know your Twitter handle?)

Hope your flight to New York went smoothly and that your meeting with the mayor was productive. Opening an office in NYC would be quite a coup! Assuming you close the deal, I can put you in touch with Pat Callahan—she's the top commercial real estate agent in the NYC area, and she can find you a great space anywhere in the five boroughs. Look forward to hearing what happened.

I'm meeting with some of the top crowdfunding people in Dallas this week to explore the possibility of some deals, and they are always asking about the latest breakthroughs in technology. May I give them your information? You may be a great resource for them.

Great to meet you—please keep in touch. Happy to help!

Best, Judy

Once you've sent your message, notice the speed of their response back to you. If they're great connectors, they'll respond to you within 24 hours, or if they don't, they'll have a great reason for waiting. (I once had to wait a week to hear from a gentleman because he was out hiking in the Wasatch Mountains and he didn't get my message. As soon as he got it, he returned the call immediately.) If you don't hear anything, you can follow up with another message or request within a week. Just make sure that your e-mail or LinkedIn request continues to be warm, with a personal touch, and it adds value.

Suppose that you have the chance to meet some prominent people (top business figures, famous speakers or entertainers, politicians, angel investors, or billionaires). Should you send them an e-mail or reach out through LinkedIn or social media? Absolutely. As Natalia Oberti Noguera, founder and CEO of Pipeline Fellowship, points out, "What's the worst that could happen if you e-mailed these people? Even if one person replies, you're better off than not having e-mailed any of them." If you are reaching out to movers and shakers, and you know the name of their assistant, send a copy of the e-mail to them as well. Always be clear that you simply wish to reconnect, not to ask a favor. If you continue to connect and add value to movers and shakers, you may be pleasantly surprised at the response. You may not be top of mind with them—yet—but adding value consistently will help move you there.

Step 2: Assess the Connections and Activate Your System

A system is a network of interdependent
components that work together.
—W. EDWARDS DEMING

Once you've sent those initial reconnection e-mails or requests, you should begin the process of assessing whether these people are good fits for your network. While I'm a firm believer that every connection has potential value for both parties, remember Dunbar's number: you have only 150 people total that you can keep up with regularly, and that includes friends and family. Think of the number of people you meet physically each year, and then add the number of professional contacts you make through e-mail, phone, LinkedIn, or other social media, and you'll quickly see that it's impossible to add all of them to your power circles or even to stay in touch with them all. Therefore, you must categorize your contacts.

There are three questions you should ask when evaluating someone new for your power circles. First, "Where did this contact come from?" I sort contacts into the following categories, in order of priority:

Someone I specifically wished to meet and perhaps reached out to in advance

An introduction from one of my power circle members

A stranger who has a connection to someone in my power circles

A stranger who has a connection to someone I know but who is not in my power circles

Someone who approaches me due to my position or skill set

Someone who approaches me in a professional setting (a conference or meeting, for example) where we are likely to have similar backgrounds and goals

A serendipitous contact in any setting (an airport or church, for example)

Anyone whom you deliberately wished to meet or anyone who was introduced to you by a power circle member should be marked as a high priority. However, any contacts may be power circle candidates due to their ecosystem or influence, or just because you like them. That's why you must ask a second question: "Do our values match?" As Warren Buffett once said, "No matter what the rate, you can't write good contracts with bad people." While it's possible that certain connections can be important even if you are not particularly in tune with their values, this question should determine whether you include these people in your power circles.

You can get a sense of someone's values in one meeting or a couple of e-mails or phone calls, but it's wise to do a little more research. Check to see if anyone in your current power circles knows him or her. Ask about this individual's reputation. Google the person, look at his or her website, and check his or her LinkedIn profile. While you may not feel the need to do this much research for a casual connection, it's worthwhile to do a little checking to avoid the pain of dealing with a bad actor.

The third question is this: "Can I provide meaningful value to them, and can they provide value to me, now and/or in the future?" While this is not the most important determiner, it is one that you should consider before you add people to your power circles. I'm all for knowing people at every age and stage of life and profession. However, for your power circles you want a group of like-minded people, with compatible values, interested in adding value to others, knowing that their success will come from mutual assistance offered in both the short and long term. In other words, you want people who have a good head, a good heart, and who are a good bet.

File Your New Connections

Based on those three questions and the responses to your reconnection e-mails, phone calls, or LinkedIn requests, you can tentatively put any connection into one of the following five "files."

Thanks but no thanks. Hopefully you will have weeded out these individuals after your first meeting. But if in the course of your research or further contact you discover that they (1) are not a good fit with your values and goals, (2) tend to take a lot without giving, or (3) are bad actors, you should mark the contacts as people to avoid if you can or to deal with cautiously if you must. You can't have users in your network because they will create damage—not just to you but to anyone you introduce them to. You must act as the gatekeeper to your power circles and do your best to keep such people out.

Informants. In the same way police use informants to gain access to information and networks closed to them otherwise, you may know individuals whose connections are excellent but with whom you need to be cautious. I have a friend who sits on a VC board with me, and she once asked me to check out a potential new funding source. The man was reputed to be very wealthy, but after I met him, several things put me on my guard. First, he claimed to have family money and a Park Avenue office, but he chose to meet me in one of those suites where you can rent an office and have access to a conference room. Second, he wasn't your typical wealthy businessman: he was missing a button on his jacket, his hair wasn't well cut, his shoes weren't shined. ... I've known a few eccentric individuals with money, but this gentleman didn't look eccentric—just unkempt. Because there seemed to be some misrepresentation, I suggested to my friend that she proceed cautiously.

While the gentleman never invested any of his own money in her fund, he did make an introduction to someone that contributed $5 million. The moral? People who may not be good candidates for your power circles may still possess valuable connections in their own networks. You wouldn't put 100 percent of your trust in these relationships, but you may be able to add and receive value as long as you are judicious, allocate your resources carefully, and make sure that any referrals or introductions made for or from these people come with a suggestion for caution.

Gray. Some people may have personality traits that are difficult. In business, you can run into tough men and women who are brusque in manner and dismissive of others, yet such people may still be valuable connections and important additions to your Vital 100. Connections are like any other relationships: if you have a good enough foundation based on sharing value (and hopefully, shared *values*), then you may be willing to put up with a few quirks and foibles. You can think of these relationships as neither black nor white but rather as inhabiting the vast area of gray. This means you may wait a while before adding them to your power circles.

Other individuals in the gray file may have what I call a low "network IQ": they don't have the value-add mentality and simply need to be educated. Whenever I refer such an individual, I'll say something like, "John has this background and may be able to help you this way, but here are a few things you should know about him up front." Then I will ask the other party to let me know how it goes.

On deck. Charlie Munger (Warren Buffett's partner and vice chairman of Berkshire Hathaway) once told a protégé that for every 100 people that he meets, 15 of them are of no interest, 5 he won't be able to live without, and 80 of them he categorizes as "wait and see."[2] Your wait-and-see numbers might be equally high when assessing potential connections. You can think of the wait-and-see people as "on deck": they may or may not become part of your power circles right now, but you will continue to stay in touch, add value, and let the relationships develop.

Power circles. These are the people who check all your boxes, so to speak. You share similar values; you like them; they have character. You feel that these relationships will provide mutual support and benefit, and you are willing to include these people in what Seth Godin calls your "tribe." Adding someone to your power circles represents new opportunities, new networks, and new relationships—people who may end up being best friends, important colleagues, and/or essential mentors.

Now you need to decide where this new connection fits in your 5+50+100 network.

Place These New Relationships in Your 5+50+100

You may already have an instinctive sense whether these individuals should be in your Key 50 or Vital 100. (Rarely do people go straight into your Top 5, as these are your closest relationships.) But it's worthwhile to do a little evaluating based on the wish list of connections you created in Chapter 6 of the people you wanted to add to your power circles to help you achieve your goals.

Look at the ecosystems where you felt you needed to know more people. Are these new contacts in any of those particular ecosystems? What strengths do they have? What levels of influence? What do you know about their networks? Your answers will determine whether you wish to add some-one to your Key 50 (important strategic relationships you're in touch with once a week) or your Vital 100 (additional contacts in important ecosys-tems, people you want to help, those you enjoy hanging out with, people whose networks are rich and significant, and those who may be good to know in the future). Remember, we are talking about *strategic* relationships, so you have to be strategic in the way you think about adding people. You are creating a community of like-minded people who will influence one another and create something greater than any of its members, so you must be intelligent about the way you build it.

Review the list of your current power circle members (see Chapter 6), and then place the new connections in the appropriate circles. Fill in as much data as you can on the new connections' ecosystems, influence levels, and so on. Using the example from Chapter 6, let's assume that this gentleman added two new people to help with his professional goal of expanding manu-facturing capacity by 40 percent. One is a factory manager, and the other is a new investor in his business. Table 8.1 shows the Key 50 and Vital 100 por-tions of his power circles (the additions are in boldface).

You'll notice one contact, Howard Finn, is in italics. Let's assume that this gentleman's child went from elementary school to middle school, and he is no longer in Mr. Finn's class (or even in the same school). Unless there is another reason to keep Mr. Finn in the Vital 100 power circle, it would be logical to move him out and perhaps put the child's new teacher in. This is natural. Clate Mask, CEO of InfusionSoft, once said, "In my mind there's a natural flow in business and in life of people moving from outer to inner circles, and that creates challenges. Because there's only so much space in the inner rings, people have to flow outwards as well." Power circles are fluid and will change over time as you grow and change, and you must be willing for members to change levels or to leave altogether. Strategic relationships are not about accumulating contacts but instead about choosing the connections that are best suited for your current circumstances, goals, and ecosystems. Adding some people to your power circles and letting others go will make it easier to focus on your relationships with the 150 people who are most important to your life and business. In Step 3, you will enrich and deepen these relation-ships by consistently adding value.

Table 8.1 Your New Power Circles: Key 50 and Vital 100

Name	Role	Location	Ecosystem or Context	Power Circle	Resources	Influence Score
Mark Starr	College room-mate	Australia	Friends	Key 50	Overseas network Real estate expert	3
Marvin Chin	Profes-sor; mentor	Chicago	Industry Friends	Key 50	Academic network Industry network	1
Patty Nathan	VC funder	San Jose	Financial	Key 50	Financial network Access to funding Expansion advice	1
Chuck Ames	Friend; golf buddy; client	Miami	Business Friend	Key 50	Community bigwig Politically connected Charities	2
Radha Shrinavas	Banker	Miami	Business Financial	Key 50	Local financial connections National financial connections	2
Bob Miller	Admin assistant	Miami	Business	Key 50	Staff connections in business Church volunteer	4
George Arica	Next door neighbor	Miami	Friends	Key 50	Real estate broker Kiwanis Arts connection	3
Tom Randall	**Investor**	**Chicago**	**Financial Industry**	**Key 50**	**VC source Expertise in overseas manufacturing**	**1**
Joe Peters	Minister	Miami	Community	Vital 100	Church Community Charity	3
Howard Finn	*Kids' teacher*	*Miami*	*Community*	*Vital 100*	*Community Sports community Academic connections*	*4*
Alice King	Local council rep	Miami	Political	Vital 100	Local Politics Community Charitable	2
Claudio Vero	Supplier	Italy	Industry	Vital 100	Industry Overseas Financial	1
Beth Veranski	**Factory manager**	**Miami**	**Industry**	**Vital 100**	**Connections with potential workers Ran a factory so knows about expansion**	**4**

Step 3: Multiply Value and Deepen the Relationship

Business relationships are just like any other relationship. They
require some effort to maintain, and they must be mutually
beneficial. As in any relationship, you must be willing
to give, share, and support, not just take or receive.

—MICHAEL DENISOFF, FOUNDER AND CEO,
DENISOFF CONSULTING GROUP

Introducing yourself is only the first step in the relationship; deep connections are built through multiple "touches" over time. Stephen M. R. Covey, author of *The Speed of Trust*, talks about making deposits in others' "trust accounts." Adding value through favors that start at a low level and progress upward and outward, from individuals through their networks, is the way to increase trust and to build authentic relationships. By basing the relationships in your power circles upon the giving and receiving of value consistently, you are establishing a strong foundation for a network that will stand the test of time.

The Four Time Frames for Following Up

To ensure that your interactions are consistent in today's busy world, you need an infallible follow-up schedule for adding value to the people in your power circles. There are four time frames to keep in mind: once a *day, week, month,* and *quarter.*

Once a day. Not only should you reconnect with any new contacts within 24 hours of your first meeting, but you always should respond to any e-mail, phone call, LinkedIn message, or other communication from people in your power circles within 24 hours. (Ideally, you should respond to communication from *anyone* within 24 hours. You never know who might be reaching out to you or whom they might have in their network.) I have found that slow follow-up is one of the three major places people fail when it comes to building strong relationships. Make it a rule to reply within 24 hours at least 95 percent of the time.

You also want to check in with your Top 5 once a day. You don't have to reach out to them every day, but because these are your closest family members and friends, you should speak with them more than once a week and have them in mind every day.

Once a week. Within seven days of contacts reaching out to you, you should send something of value. This can be an article, an introduction, a resource, an opportunity—it doesn't have to be large, but it needs to show them that you (1) have them in mind, (2) understand their goals, and (3) are committed to adding value to them consistently. A week also represents the time period in which you should connect with every one of your Key 50. Remember, these people are essential to your success, so you must keep your connections with them strong and vital.

Once a month. Every month you should reach out and add value to your Vital 100. (I do this with 25 members per week—certainly a less daunting task than all 100 at once.) If you have organized your power circles by ecosystem, it's easy to send e-mails to groups, letting them know about a particular new resource, piece of news, article or study, opportunity, or new connections. Here's an example:

To: Sue Higgins, John Peterson, Joachin Mendoza [I usually bcc everyone so it looks less like a group e-mail.]
From: Judy Robinett
Re: Thought you'd find this as fascinating as I did.

I recently saw an article on the latest trends in crowdfunding and micromanufacturing. It's incredible how 3-D printing has revolutionized the way we produce everything! Here's the link ...

I had a chance to interview the author last week, and attached are some additional insights that he didn't include in the article. If you'd like to speak with him yourself, just shoot me an e-mail and I'll connect you.

I hope to see you at the crowdfunding conference next month. Please let me know if there is anything I can do for you between now and then. Happy to help!

Best, Judy

In one e-mail I provided an article, plus an additional resource that no one else would be able to deliver. I offered to make an introduction, and I planted the seed of meeting in person the following month. You, too, can create value easily for people in your Vital 100 that share common goals, interests, and ecosystems.

Once a quarter. For the rest of the people in your Rolodex or Outlook, send out a quarterly group e-mail or LinkedIn message that features an update on your professional and personal activities and that requests that they update you as well. This is a great way to stay in the minds of people over the course of a year. I can't tell you how many times I've sent out a quarterly e-mail or LinkedIn update and gotten a response, "So glad to hear from you! I thought of you the other day when I heard about this opportunity... ." You must let others know what you are doing so they can keep you in mind.

I suggest that you set aside a specific time every week for doing your follow-up. I dedicate an hour every Friday to sending e-mails, LinkedIn messages, and making phone calls. (At 4 p.m. every Friday, ACT! and VIPorbit software cofounder Mike Muhney goes through what he calls his "touch-base orbit": a list of people he wants to contact based on events of the past week or the upcoming two weeks.) Once a quarter I set aside a Saturday morning to write and send an update e-mail to everyone in my contact files. And every time I receive a response or request from someone, I note it in my entry for that individual. I also make note of which resources I gave them, the people I introduced them to, and when they responded to my e-mail or message. This builds a rich record of all the "touches" that help to make relationships vital, and it will help you add even more value later on as you connect people within your power circles.

The Value-Add System to Build Ongoing Connection

Have you ever been given an inappropriate gift, or have you ever received help that didn't suit your needs? Have you ever had someone do you a favor and you could see the metaphoric strings attached to it? There is an art to adding value over the long term. Here are some of the secrets I have learned for multiplying value productively and building authentic relationships.

Secret 1: Add value appropriately. You need to ensure that the value you provide is suited to the recipients. What do these people need and want? What goals are they pursuing? Which of the four critical resources (opportunities, information, money, and connections) are the most important for them to reach their goals? The assistance you provide needs to be valuable in their mind. I am always e-mailing articles about topics that I know are of immediate concern to the recipients, and I often use a one-word subject line—"Validation"—and put a hyperlink in the body. When I sent one such e-mail recently to a billionaire CEO, she read the full article and called me back within 15 minutes.

The value also needs to be suited to the recipients' stage of business and capabilities. If you have an entrepreneur who's just getting started, it might not be suitable to propose him or her for a seat on a corporate board, for instance, or to offer contact details for a billionaire investor. Often the value you provide—whether it's opportunity, information, access to money, or connections—is through a contact with another member of your power circles, so it's even more important that you connect people appropriately. Every introduction represents a segment of your social capital; you don't want that social capital damaged by giving it to the wrong person or at the wrong time. Make an assessment of the person's goals, stage of life and/or business, and capabilities, and then add value in ways that will benefit him or her the most.

Secret 2: Be proactive. Ask how you can help. Giving first is rare and builds trust in a world where talk is cheap and people mistrustful, so I believe you should always provide value proactively. One of my rules is that if I can help, I will. Indeed, I end most of my e-mails or LinkedIn messages with the phrase, "Happy to help."

Some people hang back for fear that they will look like they're trying too hard. But what would you rather have: an offer for help that perhaps you can't necessarily use, or no offer of help at all? You would be surprised at how much it can mean to people if you sincerely ask how you can help with their needs and goals. Giving first is also a powerful strategy when you are trying to reach movers and shakers. One high-powered connection wrote me after I contacted her: "I thought you were too good to be true, and I wouldn't have followed up on your offer to help if you hadn't reached out first."

Even the smallest assistance given at the right time can make a big difference. Douglas S. Ellenoff, one of the founders of the law firm Ellenoff Grossman & Schole LLP (EG&S), recounts that when the firm first opened, having friends and family use their services was critical. I'm sure that for many of those people, giving their legal business to EG&S was simply a kind thing to do, but Douglas remembers it as the key to building the firm's reputation.

Secret 3: Solve their problems. Everyone has problems of some kind, and it's often difficult to see a potential solution or to access the resources you need. If you can identify what the problem is and provide a solution—by sharing relevant information, a key introduction, a piece of strategy, a referral, a mentor, or other support—you will deepen the relationship quickly.

I love adding value by solving problems. It's like a game to see how quickly I can create a solution to the issue, usually by connecting people to the resources available through my power circles. But I never hesitate to roll up my shirtsleeves and help solve the problem myself. I've volunteered for committees, helped out with campaigns, coached young entrepreneurs through their VC presentations, found board members and speakers for conferences—and, as you saw earlier, within 24 hours located a 17,000-square-foot house for an important party. Why? First, I care about others and I love to make things happen. Second, I follow the advice of actress Bette Davis, "Attempt the impossible in order to improve your work."

Secret 4: Do the little things that most people don't. In *Give and Take*, Adam Grant describes the way Silicon Valley networker Adam Rifkin does what he calls "five-minute favors," defined as any favor that takes less than five minutes. These small favors often make the biggest difference.[3] Things like sending an e-mail or text, or a message with an article ("I saw this article and thought it might be useful to you"), or calling to say, "I just met this person, and I think it would be worthwhile for the two of you to connect" lets people know you have them in mind.

One of the "biggest" little things you can do for people is to offer encouragement when they are going through challenges. A few years ago a good friend, James Benedict, was going through a tough deal negotiation, and I made a point to check in on him weekly. I'd send notes and e-mails saying,

"How are you doing? Keep going!" (something I always tell people). James has said to me repeatedly how grateful he was for my support. It takes very little time to do the little things, but their impact is often quite large. How difficult is it to send a card to say "thank you" or to mention their family or their pet at the end of a business conversation? Surprise people with small kindnesses when they least expect it, and you will be demonstrating the kind of care and concern that builds long-term trust.

Secret 5: Always do what you say you will. While this is a fundamental requirement of any authentic connection in business and in life, it's absolutely vital when it comes to multiplying value. If you say you will do something, do it, and do it by the time you say you will. If you say you'll make an introduction or that you'll let them in on an opportunity, or even just that you'll follow up by a certain time, keep your word.

Secret 6: Give without expecting a return. Value given with an expectation that you will get something in return is a transaction, not a relationship. Your goal is to do what you can for others with no strings attached and with confidence that you will be rewarded with a stronger relationship, if nothing else. However, I have found that this kind of giving without strings attached is usually rewarded, often in ways you do not expect. Author and branding consultant Dorie Clark tells a story of her early days as a freelance journalist in Boston. She got to know a local manufacturer, Steve Grossman, while she was doing a story about him. It was an excellent story, and it garnered great publicity for Mr. Grossman. Shortly afterward he announced he was running for governor. Then Dorie accepted a job as press secretary for one of his competitors. "It would have been natural for Steve to be annoyed or turn hostile in some way," Dorie said. "But he recognized that I was simply doing my job, and at every turn he was unfailingly polite." Both candidates lost in the primary, but the following year Mr. Grossman was instrumental in recommending Dorie for a top communications job in the presidential campaign of his friend, Howard Dean. When you add value freely, I believe it will always come back to you in some form—as long as you give without expectations.

Secret 7: Add value multiple times before you make any request. I once saw a quote: "Trust takes years to build, seconds to break, and forever to repair." Adding value, keeping your word, thinking about the needs of others, and doing the little things are all ways you build trust in relationships. But if you make a request before you have a healthy trust account established, all the value you've added can be discounted in a second. By adding value multiple times before you ask anything for yourself, you are establishing yourself as a "giver" in the eyes of the recipients. When they think of you, they'll think of a valued resource, someone who is helpful, caring, a problem solver, attentive to their needs, and willing to go the extra mile.

Paul C. Brunson is well known as a matchmaker (think "Hitch" only in real life), and he's had the good fortune to work with Oprah Winfrey. In a blog post, "It's Called 'Networking,' Not 'Using,'" he comments on the fact that people are constantly approaching him with products, ideas, and so on, that they want him to get to Oprah. "The biggest problem people have . . . is going for the 'ask' too soon," he writes. "The most successful relationships I have built are with people I do more for than they do for me. I give, give, give, give, give, then ask."[4] The Bible may say that it's better to give than to receive, but if you wish to build strong connections, it's essential to give, give, give, give, give, *before* you receive. A friend who is a superb networker summarizes it this way: "Get to know people; see how you can help them, and show them that you genuinely care. As the relationships deepen and others get to know you too, you'll be able to call on them for help if you need it."

When It's Time to Ask: The Quality Request That Will Gain You a "Yes"

Adding value is actually pretty enjoyable. Being the giver feels good, and it puts you in a position of strength in the relationship. If you follow the seven secrets listed above, you can be sure that you are building a strong level of trust with other people so that they feel you have their back and have their best interests at heart. However, at some point you probably will have a request to make. This is good; if a relationship is too lopsided (where one person is the only giver and the other the only taker), it can create resentment or a suffocating feeling of obligation on the other side.

Any good relationship should provide benefit to *all* parties, and the most successful people are able to provide great value to others while they also remain focused on their own goals and ambitions. Remember, in building strategic relationships, you are looking to create strong connections within specific ecosystems, with people of certain levels of influence, so that you can have their assistance in accomplishing your personal and professional goals. You need to be able to take the ask that you developed in Chapter 7 and turn it into a *quality request* that your connections will be happy to fulfill.

To make a quality request, ask yourself six questions. First, "Is this request appropriate to the person, the ecosystem, and the status of the relationship?" Don't ask a marketer for advice on a funding strategy, or a venture capitalist about marketing—wrong person *and* wrong ecosystem. (Instead, ask the marketer about the people she knows who might help with a funding strategy, and if you ask the venture capitalist about marketing, do your homework so you're sure you have the right partner.) A quality request is also appropriate to the level of connection and trust in the relationship. No one sane walks into a speed dating session with an engagement ring in his pocket, expecting to propose marriage on the spot. You should evaluate carefully whether the level of connection and trust will support your particular request.

Second, "Is this request the right size and in the right sequence?" Overasking is a mistake: it's much better to keep your requests small, especially early in the relationship. A small favor, easily granted, establishes a relationship of reciprocity and can actually increase the level of trust between you and the other person. A series of small favors asked and granted can lead easily to a much larger goal. Too many people try to go from point A to point Z rather than (1) asking for a phone call, then (2) getting a referral, then (3) asking for an introduction to that referral, then (4) asking for a follow-up phone call with the referral—all small favors, but together they lead to a new client.

Third, "Is this request strategic?" Say you're meeting with one of the leading figures in your industry. You've been adding value to her consistently, providing information, opportunities, connections, and so on. You have built a strong relationship, and your trust account with her is full. You have a goal of bringing your idea for a new product to market. What quality request will you make of her? Access to funding? Marketing advice? Connections with manufacturers? You need to think strategically in terms of who she is, what she can do for you, and where this help will fit in the journey to your goal.

Fourth, "How can I add value along with the request?" Not long ago, I sent an article to a principal at one of the top venture capital firms in the world. (I'm constantly on the lookout for articles that might be important personally or professionally for others.) In addition to the article, I sent a short summary of what I had been up to, and I asked if she and I might meet when I was next in Silicon Valley. The combination of value and quality request resulted in my being invited to Draper University when Tim Draper shared his vision with media representatives, investors, and other stakeholders. Whenever you make a quality request, try to preface it with at least one, if not more, items of value.

Fifth, "Do I have a strong 'why' for the request?" When an entrepreneur comes to me with a proposal or request for funding, I look at the business fundamentals, of course; but I'm more likely to listen if the entrepreneur is emotionally invested in the proposal and has a strong reason behind the request. People will pay more attention if they know your request is important to you and if your emotional engagement demonstrates that you have skin in the game. Energy and passion were two vital characteristics of the share you developed in Chapter 7. Bring that same energy and passion to any request you make.

Sixth, "What's my Plan B?" Even if people want to help, sometimes the answer is still "no" or "not now." Check the prep work you did before making the request (it was appropriate, the right size and sequence, strategic, you added value, and your "why" was clear), and if you feel you did everything you could, don't take the refusal personally. Always thank them for listening to your request, and then ask the questions from the last chapter: "What ideas do you have for me?" and "Who else do you know that I should talk to?" It could be that the quality request you make of one person will be fulfilled by someone he or she knows. Try making your request again at another time—after you've filled up their trust accounts with a steady stream of value.

Kay Koplovitz is a valued friend and business associate, and our relationship has been built upon the precepts of multiplying value in different ways. I had met Kay a couple of times at events of 500 or more people, and I knew she was the chairperson of Springboard Enterprises, an organization that focuses on getting women access to private capital. Now, I believed that Springboard needed to become the crowdfunding platform for women, so I sent Kay a white paper as well as further information on the topic. I then set up some conference calls with experts on the topic, and I arranged for her to meet with one of my business partners in Austin, Texas, to talk about crowdfunding. Throughout all of this, Kay and I were e-mailing and calling. I'd send her information, and she'd call and say, "I'm wondering about this." Then I'd problem solve and reply, "Those are regulatory issues so you need to talk to Galen, the attorney in New York who is the foremost expert. Let me set up a meeting." Finally, I arranged with my friend, Leo Hopf, to donate a day of his time to meet with Kay and a few of the other top people at Springboard. At the end of the day, the session proved to be a game changer for the organization.

Not long after this, I was on a panel at a conference in New York, and Kay came to see me speak. Afterward, she sat next to me at the table reserved for speakers. As we chatted, there were several people waiting to speak with Kay, and she turned to one of them and said, "Judy's my advisor." That was a very public acknowledgment and a testament to the relationship we had built over time. Kay herself says that she can't remember the first time she met me: "It seems as if there was a moment in time when all of a sudden Judy showed up and was very active in what we were doing. She's a consummate connector and is enormously generous with sharing information that's interesting to you, and she follows up with it and is incredibly generous in connecting people who would be useful for Springboard."

When you focus on building your relationships by consistently adding value, you are setting a foundation for mutual aid and assistance between you and other people. You are also setting the tone for your entire network. In *Connected*, Nicholas Christakis and James Fowler point out that altruism— the ability to contribute to others without necessarily expecting anything in return—and reciprocity—the desire to give back when someone has given to you—are key traits of most successful social networks. When you add value consistently, time after time, and you show people that keeping them in mind is important to you, then that kind of attitude will quickly become the norm for your power circles, and for anyone who joins them. And they, too, will experience the enjoyment and richness that giving freely to others can bring.

Phase 4: Connect Your Connections for Added Success

....

*When you make those human connections, you automatically
see and clear away obstacles that stand between you and the flow
of resources—and once the obstacles fall, resources naturally
tend to flow toward good ideas and worthy projects.*

—JENNIFER MCCREA AND JEFFREY C. WALKER,
THE GENEROSITY NETWORK

Phase 4 separates a power connector from an ordinary networker
because power connectors are experts at linking people to create the
maximum benefit for all concerned. They love figuring out which
contact can be most helpful, how X can add value to Y, and how connecting
both with Z can increase that value exponentially. Author of *Laughing at Wall
Street*, Chris Camillo, describes just such a power connector:

> *When I was a young business development professional, a senior colleague
> of mine, Billy Payton, taught me the importance of relationship building.
> I could hand him a brief of a company's board of directors and man-
> agement team, and within minutes he'd locate a strong connection with
> someone in his network—and this was before the emergence of LinkedIn.
> Even more astonishing to me was how responsive and receptive his contacts
> were to his requests for help. People remembered Billy, and they liked him.*

He always gave more than he took from his relationships, yet was never too proud to ask for what he wanted. You can be great at whatever it is that you do, but it is the breadth, depth, and quality of relationships with others that will determine your sphere of influence and ultimate success.

Chris's mentor, Billy Payton, demonstrates the advantages of being a power connector in the world of business. That advantage is a combination of the connector's skills, the depth and richness of his or her power circles, and most of all, the ability to facilitate linkages between and among power circle members and their networks. Author Bob Burg understands the power of being the one who connects the connectors. "Position yourself as a center of influence, the one who knows the movers and shakers," he says. "People will respond to that, and you'll soon become what you project."

We talked earlier in Chapter 2 about strong links versus weak links and how a combination of both produces the healthiest networks. But in Phase 4, we are moving beyond networks and linkages into *collaboration* and *cooperation*. In the same way that adding value multiple times deepens a business relationship, cooperation and collaboration deepen connections within your power circles. Instead of $1 + 1 = 2$, connections within your power circles produce results that are more like $1 + 1 = 3$, or even $1 + 1 = 11$.[1] To connect your connections effectively, however, you must first draw a map—a matrix of who is in your power circles and how they are (or could be) linked to one another.

Step 1: Map the Links Between Your Connections

> Think about how much money and time goes into a company
> CRM to track their enterprise relationships. If relationships are
> important to your business, you need to do the same.
> —LEE BLAYLOCK, FOUNDER OF WHO@

As a politician, Lyndon Johnson (LBJ) knew how to get things done. He was a U.S. senator for 12 years, 10 of them in leadership positions (majority leader, minority leader, and majority whip). As president, he shepherded through Congress legislation that protected civil rights, established Medicare and Medicaid, increased aid to education and environmental protection, and launched the War on Poverty. LBJ was known for his ability to strong-arm reluctant colleagues—but his real expertise lay in knowing which colleagues to coerce.

He used to map out which politicians were involved in the process of passing a particular bill. He'd track the bill's progress and apply what was called the "Johnson treatment" to any reluctant supporters. Because he had a clear map, LBJ knew exactly where the inflection points were located in these particular *value chains*. Your goal is to have an equally clear map of the value inflection points for your power circles—meaning, where people can connect to produce more value for one another. Without a map, you will have to work hard to figure out who's connected to whom and how best to hook up X to Y. With a map, you can shortcut the process significantly.

The Mapping Process

A power circles map resembles a social network analysis map, or LinkedIn's InMap feature (which tracks how your various LinkedIn contacts are connected to each other). While I use InMap, I also use a combination of mind mapping software and old-fashioned sticky notes on a wall to draw the connections in my own power circles. In the Resources section at the end of this book, you'll find a list of mapping tools and websites. But no matter which tool you use, there are some basic categories of information you want to capture in your map. Here's the process:

1. Have at hand all the contact information for each person in your power circles. This will include your notes on where you met them, who introduced you, how you have been in touch with them, who works with them, and so on.

2. Take the chart you updated in Chapter 8 to include any additions to your power circles.

3. Start with your Top 5 power circle. Put the name of each member in the middle of a page, and underneath the name put the different ecosystems of which he or she is a part. An example from the charts in Chapters 6 and 8 would look like this:

4. Now, look at the rest of your power circles and see who else is linked to this person, and draw the connections. Use different colors for the different ecosystems. Here's our example:

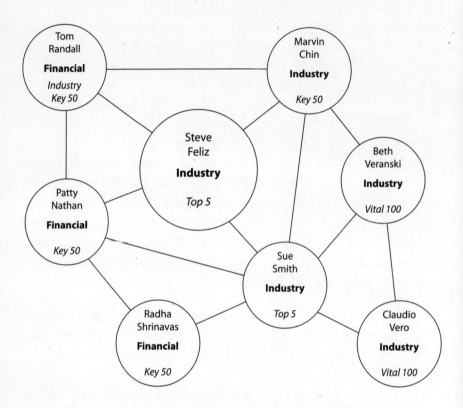

This map was done with a Top 5 member in the middle, but you can do a map for yourself, a map by ecosystem, a map by relationship chain (Tom introduced you to Jane, who introduced you to Connie, who introduced you to Hwan), a map by industry, a map by region or physical location—whatever kinds of relationships it would benefit you to map, you can. Here's a map of the chain of introductions that led to my meeting Heidi Roizen and Meg Whitman. You'll notice that both individuals and conferences are part of this map; you can do the same with your introduction maps, as we'll discuss in Chapter 10.

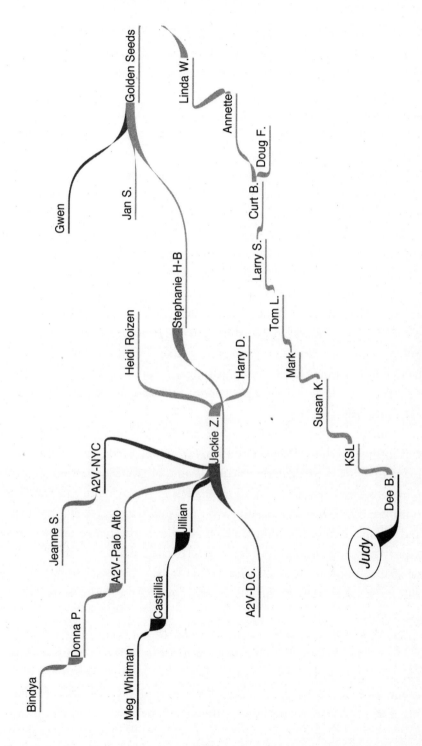

Relationship maps are useful in several ways. First, you'll see how much your power circle members are interlinked. You want to have a healthy degree of connection and overlap, and you also want to have some people who are on the periphery, to be conduits of new connections and ecosystems you could not otherwise access.

Second, you'll see where the holes are in your network and where you might seek to add more people. Is your network local, regional, national, international? Are you strong in some ecosystems and weak in others? Who in your power circles could help you add members to increase your presence in key ecosystems and areas? You'll also notice where you may be missing information on your connections. Do you recall how you met these individuals, and who was the original contact? Whenever possible, fill in missing details.

Third, you'll understand how one relationship can lead to another and another and another. ... When I did this exercise, I discovered that 40 people in my power circles originated from just one introduction. Entrepreneur Robyn Scott once did a similar exercise, and she found more than 60 intros had led her to people like Archbishop Tutu and the Dalai Lama. "Connectors hold the keys, through their introductions, to incredible value, locked up in networks," she writes.[2]

Fourth, you'll start to notice the relationship potential within your current connections. Who in your power circles needs to know another member? This is particularly valuable if one of your connections is stepping into a new venture or location. If a friend is moving to San Francisco from the East Coast, for example, you can pull out your Bay Area "map" and set up a series of introductions. If another business associate wants to expand his company and your financial ecosystem map is healthy, you may be able to put him in touch with people to help him get funding. Being able to see such relationships at a glance will make you a better power connector.

Fifth, you'll be able to see the other power connectors in your circles. Some may be obvious, but others may surprise you. In the six degrees of separation experiment I mentioned in Chapter 3, the most important link in the chain between Omaha and a stockbroker in Boston was the owner of a clothing store in Sharon, Massachusetts.[3] People can be power connectors due to their prominence, their level of influence, the resources they have access to, or by the sheer variety and intensity of their connections with others. Others have developed an expertise in linking different people together, or perhaps they are a hub between ecosystems (a financial expert or investor who also writes a column for *Forbes*, for example; or the minister who serves on the board of the state arts council). Power connectors can provide shortcuts for everyone in your network to reach the people who may be critical to their success.

As you build your maps, you can use them to capture other important information on your power circle members—their goals, their contacts, the favors you've done for them, the connection points they have added as a result of your efforts to put them in touch with key individuals. Between the relationship map, your power circle spreadsheet, and the data you capture in your contact info software, you should have a very clear picture of the people and the relationships within your power circles. Then, you should be able to incorporate new connections efficiently and effectively.

Adding New Connections

Whenever you add contacts to your power circles, you also should add them to your connection maps. But first, you need to gather as much information about them as you can. See if you can answer the following questions about anyone you are adding to your power circles. If not, spend some time to get to know them better:

◆ *About them.* What are their strengths? What are their goals? What ecosystems are they already in? What diversity of experience and/ or ecosystem will they add to your power circles? People who bring new elements to your power circles will enrich them, often by more than a factor of one. Former venture capitalist turned tech entrepreneur Erin Valenti comments, "Getting help from the right person at the right time is one of the biggest problems startups face because teams are so small and resources are so constrained. I've been able to mitigate some of those issues by building hundreds of relationships with people with all sorts of diverse backgrounds and skill sets."

◆ ***About their connections.*** Every new contact adds an entirely new network to your power circles. Who is in their network? What level of influence do they have within it? How far can you trace their connections within their network? Remember the power of weak links: the resource you or someone in your power circles needs may be five links away in this new individual's network.

◆ ***About their associations.*** In what groups and organizations do they participate, and what are their roles? Recently entrepreneur Lisa Curtis described working with several different groups to launch a $50,000 crowdfunding campaign via social media. "Organizations make even better ambassadors because they often have much bigger networks than individuals," she says.[4] Groups and organizations often will open entirely new ecosystems to you and your power circles. One of my newer connections invited me to stay at the Union Club in New York City when I was attending a conference there. The Union Club counts several former U.S. presidents as well as top CEOs in its membership, and the *only* way you can gain access is by invitation from a member. Groups and associations allow you to connect efficiently with large numbers of people in specific ecosystems.

Take the information about new connections and add it to your contact file. As you learn more, you will start to see the possibilities for you and your power circles to add value to this new contact, and for him or her to add value to your network. To start the process, ask the following questions:

Which contacts do they already know in your power circles? Which power circle members should you connect them with immediately?

What ecosystems do they need to access? Which members of your power circles are in those ecosystems?

Which of your power circle members' groups and associations do they need to reach and/or join?

Which other contacts in their network might your power circle members (or you) like to get to know?

Which of their groups and associations could open doors for you or your power circle members?

All of these questions can be condensed into one that I heard recently from Wing Lam, the co-owner of a local Wahoo's Fish Tacos restaurant: "Who do you know, and what can you do for them?" In most circumstances, your help will take the form of connecting people with others—in particular, other individuals in your power circles.

Step 2: Play 3-D Power Chess—Link People Within Your Power Circles

> Social connections are essentially the original Internet, connecting
> different pockets of intelligence to make each pocket more than it
> would otherwise be by itself.
>
> —MATTHEW D. LIEBERMAN,
> *SOCIAL: WHY OUR BRAINS ARE WIRED TO CONNECT*

I love connecting people I know with new resources within my power circles. I am constantly reaching out to my network for suggestions to help someone achieve their ends. But instead of thinking linearly—let me introduce Sam to Suzie who knows how to do X—connecting people is more like playing 3-D chess. I look at different relationships on different levels, which enables me to see how one move can produce success for many different people. I link Sam to Carolyn, whose network includes Paul, who works with Doris, who is the very person that Sam needs to meet.

My good friend Jeff Jagard (who is a vice president at a global wealth management firm) introduced me to Sunnie Giles, a former Accenture consultant who recently moved to Utah. The same week another friend introduced me to a successful serial entrepreneur who was relocating to Park City, Utah. Both Sunnie and the entrepreneur asked if I would help them develop connections in the area. That week Jeff invited Sunnie and me to a professional dinner that featured many of the movers and shakers in the area, so I asked if he would also include the entrepreneur. At the dinner, several new relationships were formed that resulted in board seat offers, funding for a new venture, and new client relationships—and both Sunnie and the entrepreneur met a large number of important people in the local area. This kind of power connecting is a strategic approach where better connections lead to better opportunities and greater resources for all concerned.

The 3-D chess game is based on a sequence of *what, why, who,* and *how. What* do they want or need? *Why* do they want it? *Who* can help them? And *how* can you put them together with the people they need? Many people don't do this kind of planning or strategizing when it comes to their connections: they know *what* they want, but not the rest. In that case, I help them get clear on the outcome by working backward from the result; then I can figure out the resources they need and come up with a strategy to reach them. I believe that everybody always needs something, and for every need, there's always a match. My job is to help figure out what that match is and how to foster the connection. I make it a game—to find the best matches and create what I call *value-plus* (value on both sides).

Many people just need to be connected to the right resources, and all it takes is an e-mail introduction and they can move on from there. Other times you may connect them to more than one resource. The ultimate goal, however, is not to connect them with a lot of people, but with the *right* people. Lewis Schiff, executive director of the Inc. Business Owners Council, surveyed 800 business owners to determine their strategies for success. In his research, 96 percent of the business owners whose companies were worth more than $30 million believed that "knowing the right people" mattered in their success. "Knowing five people who know five people goes a lot further than 5,000 LinkedIn friends," Schiff commented.[5] In other cases, the right connection is with an organization or association. One of the keys to success is to join groups that will provide access to whatever people might need—contacts, resources, opportunities, funding, and so on. When I first moved to Utah, I was asked by someone to be on a finance committee for a politician, and at a committee meeting, I met a woman who ran the Salt Lake Film Festival, who asked me to join that organization. Through both of those groups I met most of the well-connected people in Salt Lake, including five billionaires.

Sometimes the best match in your 3-D chess game is with a power connector whose large network can lead to someone who can fill the need. Author Iyanla Vanzant told me, "I don't know everybody, but my friend Susan does. I will call Susan, let her know what my vision is, and she puts me in touch with her people. And I treat them well because I know I have access to them because of Susan." Brad Thatcher founded Thatcher+Co., a strategic communications firm, in July 2008—right at the beginning of one of the worst economic cycles in U.S. history. He managed to survive and thrive because of his connections with clients and with other communications specialists. "Having a deep network of contacts at potential clients and with industry professionals that can become employees is at the heart of succeeding in a service business like mine," he says. "Without those relationships, I don't have a business." A true power connector can put almost anyone in touch with the person he or she needs within just a few contacts, and usually those doors will fly open when the power connector makes the introduction.

When you are on the receiving end of an introduction, however, it's important to avoid making unintentional mistakes that can inadvertently sour the connection. Here are five of the most common mistakes I see.

Mistake 1: Assuming an uninspiring initial e-mail or phone conversation means that it's not worthwhile to pursue the relationship. Not long ago I wanted to introduce a financial consulting group to a member of my power circles, who responded that she didn't have time to hear their "pitch," and she would do a phone call first to see if there was any chemistry. However, there is never as much chemistry over the phone or e-mail as there is in an in-person meeting. If you think this is a connection worth pursuing, or if it's a referral from a valued resource, try to meet face-to-face.

Mistake 2: Keeping yourself in the "box" of your assumptions about a potential resource. Because the woman in the above example is in an associated industry, I thought that a meeting with these financial consultants might produce sparks of creativity that would benefit all parties concerned. You must get outside of the trap of your assumptions and be open to possibilities beyond the obvious.

Mistake 3: Not trusting the person who is making the introduction. Most power connectors are extremely careful about the people they choose to introduce to one another. I'm cautious about the quality of people I refer, and

I will never waste my time and/or contacts if I can avoid it. If someone that you respect introduces you to a new contact, respect the introducer enough to explore the relationship.

Mistake 4: Not following through on an introduction. It's astonishing to me how many people will tell me they want something, but when I tell them, "Call so-and-so, I'll introduce you," they don't follow through. Remember, each introduction represents a piece of someone's valuable social capital, as well as being the key to your goals. Do the power connector the courtesy of following through promptly, and let him or her know the result of the introduction. As media entrepreneur Elisa All comments, "The people who make an introduction are putting themselves out there for you, so you be sure to make them proud. Always make them look smart for having made the introduction, and then thank them and nurture those relationships."

Mistake 5: Failing to keep critical players in the loop. I once introduced a gentleman to a friend at a major VC firm, and while the gentleman pursued the relationship, he kept me out of the conversational loop. This is a twofold problem. First, it's important for me to know how the relationship is developing so I can see if there is anything else I can do to support either party. Second, keeping the power connector in the loop keeps him or her top of mind for both parties and strengthens all three relationships. And it's just possible that the power connector may have other contacts that can be of even more assistance. Consider it a courtesy to keep the power connector informed of the progress of the relationship he or she helped to initiate.

By connecting people within your power circles with each other, you are increasing the strength of each member and promoting a culture of adding value and helping others. One particular form of connection is a favorite of mine, because it (1) adds massive value, (2) strengthens connections between people significantly, and (3) increases the chances that people will continue to connect even when I'm not there. I call this *creating a power triangle.*

Step 3: Activate Power Triangles—You + Two = Success

I am always motivated to make the right connections for people,
and my rich circle of business connections allows me to do just
that. No matter what folks need, I want to be the one that
makes that happen.

—DENISE BROSSEAU

Two years ago I met Jeanne Sullivan, founder of Starvest VC, at a meeting of
the Alley to the Valley (A2V), a key association that brings together important women in the financial ecosystem. At a subsequent meeting in New
York, I left my suitcase in Jeanne's office while we attended the last session
of a conference. When I came by to get the suitcase, Jeanne had Claudia
Iannazzo in her office. Jeanne introduced us and said we ought to know each
other, so before I left, Claudia and I sat down and talked for 20 minutes.
I listened closely to discover who she is, what interests her, and where she
is going in life. (As a result of our initial conversation, Claudia and I are
now working on deals together.) A few months later, Claudia was asked by
Baylene Wacks to find a speaker for a big entrepreneurs' conference in
New York City. Claudia reached out to me, and I put her in touch with
Dr. Annette McClellan, who had just sold her company for several million
dollars and was looking around for her next opportunity. Annette spoke at
the conference and was a great hit.

This is an example of *triangulation*, where a power connector creates
value for multiple parties at the same time. Baylene found a great speaker;
Claudia was able to help a good friend and professional contact; Annette
received great exposure to entrepreneurs and companies in which she might
invest; and I was able to help two friends as well as add a contact (Baylene) in
a new ecosystem (professional speaking). As a power connector, some of your
greatest successes will come not necessarily from being part of the relationship
yourself but rather from being the "matchmaker" between connections. After
all, even if you are incredibly efficient with your networking, you only have so
much time and so many resources in a given day. But if you can connect your
connections to one another, you are adding value while increasing the density
of your network—and according to Metcalfe's law (the theory behind why

the Internet and companies like Facebook work), the denser the network, the greater its value.[6] With triangulation, once you've made an introduction, you can step out, knowing that value is being created without your being there. You're leveraging your time and energy by using the resources of those in your network.

Here are four keys to successful triangulation.

Connect people across ecosystems. According to Christakis and Fowler, there is greater than a 50 percent probability that any two of your social contacts know each other.[7] And at higher levels of business and most professions, it's even more likely that the top people are connected. (Most thought leaders and prominent individuals are power connectors themselves.) In other words, the "old boys' network" is alive and well.

However, you can set yourself apart as a power connector by triangulating people across ecosystems. A simple version of this is opening up your local Rolodex to someone who is just moving to town and needs access to the local ecosystem. A more sophisticated example is the way I found my literary agent. Marvin Acuna is a movie producer for whom I helped find a house in Park City for a party. I mentioned to him that several of my connections thought I should write a book on strategic relationships, and he said, "You have to call Wendy Keller—she's a great literary agent." I had no contacts in the publishing world, but my connections in entertainment led to Wendy and the book business ecosystem. If you have good diversity of ecosystems in your power circles, you can add significant value by connecting people from one ecosystem to the other, providing access that they would have difficulty attaining otherwise.

Connect people from different levels while always asking, "What's in it for them?" The more successful you are, the more you need access to quality people. And those who are newer in their professions and ecosystems are eager to meet movers and shakers. As a power connector, you are in a great position to link the successful with the up-and-coming, but you must do so intelligently. As business communications expert Ronna Lichtenberg remarks, "Some of my friends have done well in the world, and folks often ask me for intros to them. If I can't think of why the intro would be helpful or welcome to my friend, I won't make the intro."

Most of those who are seeking the attention of movers and shakers never think of the relationship from the movers and shakers' point of view. Instead, they must ask the question, "What's in it for them?" and keep in mind the fundamental principle of power connecting: add value first, add value consistently, and make sure the value you add is appropriate for the other person.

Solve their problems. Better yet, anticipate their needs. Every person has some kind of problem, and everyone can offer some kind of solution. However, power connectors go beyond reactively solving problems by proactively anticipating people's needs. This is part of the "add value first" focus of power connectors. Put yourself in other people's shoes, and figure out what you can do to help them achieve their goals.

Find value that benefits all parties. The first time I attended an Alley to the Valley conference, I found myself next to a woman I didn't know, so I introduced myself. It turned out she had been one of the first venture capitalists in Silicon Valley, and she knew *everybody*. I noticed that throughout the session this woman was texting Bill Gates. I finally asked her, "What's going on?"

She said, "Paul Allen, Bill Gates's former partner at Microsoft, just released a book, and there's some really negative stuff in it."

I told her, "Text him, 'Everything you do says who you are, not to worry.' And I have a book that might be of help: *Rethink, Reinvent, Reposition: 12 Strategies to Renew Your Business and Boost Your Bottom Line*. It's on business strategy, and it was written by my friend Leo Hopf."

So I called Leo (who lived in the area) and asked if he could bring me a copy of his book for Bill Gates. Leo signed a copy, brought it to me, and I gave it to this woman to give to Bill. It made Leo's day to get his book into Bill Gates's hands; it made the woman happy to provide a resource to Bill that he might not have known about; and it made me happy that I could connect three great people by adding value to each of them.

That's an example of something I call a *value chain*. Here's another example: while working on this book, I contacted several other authors whose material I liked, and I then introduced them to each other via this e-mail:

To: Jeffrey C. Walker, Adam M. Grant, and Rich McKeown

Dear Jeff, Adam, and Rich,

Please note the stats below related to trust and governance of PE firms and their GPs and LPs. Each of you references this in your books.

Rich, meet Adam, who authored *Give and Take*, and Jeff, who is coauthor of *The Generosity Network*. Adam's concept of takers fits well with your concept of empty faces at the table. Jeff will identify with Mike's story at dinner of the rodeo star who described life as broncos' bucking, bulls' kicking, and he was willing to do the hard work but needed funding. Jeff has a superb section on bringing people together to create solutions in the philanthropy space and tossing aside issues of fear and scarcity (a little less than $300 billion donated in 2011).

Rich is coauthor of *Finding Allies, Building Alliances*, which explains how a well-chosen network can become a powerful alliance. Clay Christensen wrote the intro, and Mike Leavitt is Rich's business partner and coauthor.

I'm just delighted to know you! Have a wonderful weekend with your families and friends.

Best, Judy

Who knows if these gentlemen will ever collaborate on anything? But could they be potential endorsers, resources, and expert references for one another? Absolutely. By connecting them with one another in a power triangle, I am providing value across the board while strengthening my own relationship with all three.

Step 4: Power Connectors Do What It Takes to Make the Connection Work

> Never take your professional relationships for granted. Support them and treat them with care. They have amazing power when treated with the respect they deserve.
>
> —ELISA ALL

Human beings are wired to connect and form alliances, to cooperate and collaborate, and to support one another. Therefore, you should put time and effort into helping others through your connections and resources. *Power connectors do everything possible to make their connections work.* As you interact with your power circle members, keep updating and enriching your relationship maps, power circle charts, and contact software, so you can help them reach the right person, with the right skill, in the right ecosystem, for their needs.

Share your knowledge, contacts, articles, books, and critical information on trends, as well as access to funding, key opinion leaders, potential clients and contracts, referrals, investors, other key people, new deals, and board opportunities. The more you help people, the more you will learn about their needs, problems, solutions, talents, strengths, and abilities, and the easier it will be to help connect them with others who can help them attain their goals. And if you can't find a resource in your power circles, undoubtedly one of your connections will be able to lead you to it. Leveraging both people and information across your network is an irresistible combination that builds deep and lasting relationships.

The best power connectors create an environment of generosity and contribution among all members, where people can ask for what they need and add the value they have to offer. Sometimes asking for help is tough, and some of us find it difficult to admit we need it. But when you build an environment of generosity and mutual support within your power circles, asking and giving simply become two sides of the coin and interchangeable roles—today I give, tomorrow I receive. And that kind of atmosphere turns a group of individuals into a community with a culture of helping others. Such a community makes it easier to access any resource you need and create the kind of connections that outsiders call "lucky breaks" but insiders understand are just the result of the desire to help. You'll find that you can ask almost anything from your network, and you'll get the exact resource you need on the first try.

Congressman Paul Ryan once said, "Every successful individual knows that his or her achievement depends on a community of persons working together." Your power circles are just such a community; and as you link members and help them to add value generously, among and with one another, you will find that your own power and influence—and better yet, fulfillment—increase exponentially as well.

10

Power Connecting Strategies for Social Media and Conferences

The digital revolution and societal shifts have brought us to a
new period. It is called the Relationship Era.
—BOB GARFIELD AND DOUG LEVY,
CAN'T BUY ME LIKE

I t used to be that the only way we could meet people was face-to-face—
an introduction from a friend or colleague, or an encounter at a meeting, on the street, or in a group setting. Today there are other important
avenues where you can actively seek to build strategic relationships.[1] In an
Ipsos Observer 2012 study of over 1,000 businesspeople and small business
owners in the United States, over half of those surveyed mention using the
Internet, parties, conferences, and community functions as primary networking locations.[2]

Both conferences and the Internet allow you to reach people you would
find hard to connect with otherwise and to tap into ecosystems where you
have few, if any, resources or references. Power connectors must know how
to extend their networks effectively by utilizing both electronic media and
face-to-face contact—new school and old school—to build stronger strategic
connections across the board.

Crowd Networking: How Power Connectors Connect Online

The Internet is becoming the town square for the global village of tomorrow.
—BILL GATES

Remember the six degrees of separation? According to a 2012 study, with the advent of the Internet and social networking, most people are now separated by only 3.74 "intermediaries."[3] In this digital age we are constantly connected: we can videoconference or hold electronic meet-ups on Skype and Google+, follow friends and thought leaders on Twitter as well as their blogs, and keep up with people on LinkedIn and Facebook. With the potential to connect with any of 1.9 billion users on Facebook, 259 million on LinkedIn, 540 million on Google+, and 500 million on Twitter (all numbers as of fall 2013),[4] it has never been as easy to reach anyone, anywhere, anytime. International business magnate Richard Branson commented, "Just recently, a 12-year-old business studies student sent me an e-mail asking for some tips, and I spotted her note and wrote back."[5]

The Internet has formalized and expanded the power of the kinds of weak ties that are so important to a healthy network. With the click of a button, you can reach people who are completely unlike you and bring greater diversity to your network. You can participate in wide-ranging communities and share information, news, opinions, and resources. By sending messages, tweeting and retweeting, blogging, commenting on others' blogs, and participating in LinkedIn groups and discussion boards, you can keep yourself top of mind with your network and perhaps with thought leaders in your particular industry. You can even put your money where your heart is, by contributing to social causes or funding new business ventures. Entrepreneurship and fundraising have been completely disrupted by online crowdfunding. Reaching large groups of individual investors is possible only because of our "Internetworked" world.

With all the attention paid to networking online and its speed and ability to reach around the world in nanoseconds, it's easy to forget that our tweets, e-mails, text messages, blogs, or posts cannot take the place of real, human, face-to-face connections. Power connectors understand that they need to focus not just on the frequency or convenience of connecting online but also on communicating the kind of sharing and caring, warmth and competence that are the foundation of every real connection. Remember, the goal is a network that is wide and deep but also *robust*, meaning interconnected and responsive. And robustness comes only with consistent, caring communication.

There are five fundamental channels that power connectors currently use to create and maintain relationships online: LinkedIn; e-mail; Twitter; content creation and commentary; and Facebook. With the speed of innovation, undoubtedly there will be many more such channels in the future, and power connectors should keep abreast of trends to take advantage of these new avenues of communication. Let's see how you can use social media and an online presence to (1) maintain strong relationships with power circle members, (2) reach out to people referred to you by your contacts, and (3) target and connect effectively with people you wish to reach, especially the movers and shakers in different ecosystems.*

Online Tool 1: LinkedIn

> If everyone in the country understood how to use LinkedIn,
> it would raise the GDP.
>
> —REID HOFFMAN, FOUNDER OF LINKEDIN

Among the existing professional online connection tools, LinkedIn is the biggest and the most important in use today. LinkedIn and Twitter users tend to have larger networks (and net worths) than most Americans.[6] Because it was built to foster business networking, LinkedIn is filled with tools that can help you keep engaged with your power circles, meet their connections, and contact people you don't know but you feel would be beneficial to add to your network. In a 2013 survey of LinkedIn users, 61.8 percent rated LinkedIn as "extremely important" or "very important" when it comes to growing their networks, developing their businesses, or finding employment.[7]

---

*Please note: This book is not designed to give you tutorials in the basics of LinkedIn, Twitter, Facebook, blogging, and so on. You can find great information on all of those topics online or in books available through Amazon.com. See the Resources section at the end of this book for some suggestions.

LinkedIn is organized around three levels of connections: the people you know (first degree), the people they know (second degree), and the people those people know (third degree). You add to your LinkedIn network by inviting people and by accepting invitations from others. While more than 40 percent of LinkedIn users have between 300 and 1,000 connections,[8] it's unlikely that they can have real relationships with all of them. Investment fund founder Nadine Terman comments, "Just because someone 'links' to 1,000 people, it does not mean that he or she can really count on that network. It has to be based on a solid relationship." Even on LinkedIn, it's better to have deep connections with a small number of people, so you can actually reach out to them and add value on a regular basis.

Most of your power circle members should be part of your first-level connections on LinkedIn, and you should make yourself familiar with their profile pages, as you may discover things about them that you didn't know (where they attended college and their special skills, interests, professional awards, and so on). LinkedIn allows you to provide three different kinds of ongoing value to your power circle members. First, you may know someone they need to know, and you can easily provide an introduction or connection through LinkedIn.

Second, remember the relationship map that you drew in Chapter 9? The real power of your power circles lies not only in their relationship with you but also in their interconnections with one another. On LinkedIn, it's easy for you to link different power circle members with one another simply by providing an introduction or a recommendation that X send Y an invitation. However, be judicious with your LinkedIn introductions. If you make an introduction, you want to be sure it will be welcomed because (1) it's a good match and (2) there is value for both parties.

Third, LinkedIn's greatest potential comes from its ability to expand your network by connecting you with people you do not know and may never have the chance to meet in the normal course of business. It's often in the second- and third-degree connections of the people in your network where you will find the kinds of weak links that can provide entry into new ecosystems. Look at the networks of your power circles, and if there is someone you wish to know, request a LinkedIn introduction to them. Whenever you can, "triangulate" connections between the networks of your power circle members by suggesting that the business valuation expert that Y has in his network, for example, is exactly the resource that Z needs as she prepares to sell her company.

Even if someone is not connected to your network, you still can use LinkedIn to reach that person. This is a great way to connect with movers and shakers in different ecosystems. Start by looking up their profiles to see if any of your first-, second-, or third-degree connections are linked with them already. If so, you can connect through the members you have in common. If not, see which LinkedIn groups they belong to and whether the groups are closed (members must be approved before being allowed to join) or open (anyone can join). Group members can send messages to one another even if they have not accepted an individual's request to connect. Most LinkedIn groups are formed around a particular topic, interest, or commonality. If the group is closed, you must join the group before you reach out to any specific member, and then add value promptly and consistently by participating in discussions, posing and answering questions, welcoming new members, and so on.

There's an old saying that you are judged by the company you keep, and while you are the only one who knows the identities of the members of your power circles offline, people who look at your LinkedIn profile can see the caliber of those who are one degree away from you. In the same way that your power circle members are some of your most important business resources, your LinkedIn network has the potential to be an equally valuable asset. Therefore, you want to choose it carefully, share it judiciously, and add value to it frequently.

Keep track of the people you are connected to on LinkedIn, and be selective in terms of the requests you make and accept. Keep your profile open so you can receive "connect" requests from people you don't know, and then assess the contacts with the steps outlined in Chapter 8. In particular, look at who is and isn't on their lists of connections and recommendations. Not long ago a gentleman I met at a conference requested that I add him on LinkedIn. I noticed that even though he claimed he had received a multi-million-dollar exit package from his company, the only person who recommended him was one vendor. If he had left on good terms, you would expect a linkage to or recommendation from the CEO or board of directors. I decided not to accept his invitation.

Whenever you send or respond to a LinkedIn request, whether it is to someone who is connected to your power circle members or someone you wish to bring into your network, start building trust immediately by what I call a "warm" response—one that establishes commonality and makes an offer to add value (or adds value immediately if appropriate). Here's an example of an exchange following a LinkedIn request I received from a stranger.

From: Judy Robinett

Hi Gabriela,

I carefully reviewed your LinkedIn profile and am also familiar with your industry. But most importantly, I support women leaders whom I judge to have a bright future. You fit that category nicely, and you reached out to me, which shows me you are interested in building a robust network—globally. Your net worth will equal your network. Everything is attached to people; funding, opportunities, knowledge, and support.

A few years ago I gave a speech in Madrid and loved my visit! Let me know if there is anything I can help you with.

Best, Judy

The key to building a strong LinkedIn network is to treat every member just as you would any connection: keep adding value multiple times, offer to do what you can to be of help, and keep strengthening the relationship by your continual engagement.

Online Tool 2: E-mail

I send e-mails all the time because it's one of the easiest tools available for reaching out to people. Even the movers and shakers who aren't on LinkedIn (or who have people to manage their LinkedIn accounts) have at least one, if not several, e-mail addresses. And since most people get e-mail on their smartphones, you can reach anyone, anywhere, almost anytime. I use e-mail to send valuable information, suggest connections, and to make introductions. (See the "triangulation" e-mail in Chapter 9.) The key, however, is to make sure that your e-mail stands out.

For your power circle members, the fact that the e-mail came from you should carry some weight. For new people you wish to connect with, you must create some "non-salesy" intrigue in your subject line. You can use a common point of reference ("Re: We met at the TEDx conference—here's the info on crowdfunding you asked me for") or relationship ("Re: Paul Davis asked me to give you this"). Often when I e-mail someone to establish a relationship, I will include the name of the person who gave me the contact's name or the place where I met the contact, why I think it would be great for us to connect, a bit about me and my story, a very relevant resource or other piece of value, and then a question to get a dialogue going. E-mail is an incredibly easy way to provide value in the form of information, introductions, advice, expertise, and expressions of care about things that are important to recipients.

Online Tool 3: Twitter

With Twitter, power connectors can add value to their networks *and* reach out to thought leaders they wish to know. You can tweet content, share links you find interesting and/or important, comment on news, and get your opinion out to a broad network. By retweeting others' content, you can add value to them while getting yourself on their radar for your contribution.

One of the most effective uses of Twitter is to gain access to what I call *expert strangers*: people you wish to connect with but don't yet know. I have used Twitter to connect with authors in my areas of expertise, and I have discovered that they love to share their research and insights. (This was how I became connected with Jennifer Abernethy, author of several books on social media marketing.) Select key authors, industry figures, or those who are prominent in the particular ecosystems you wish to enter, and follow them on Twitter. Add value to them by retweeting their posts to your network and asking appropriate and knowledgeable questions.

You also can position yourself as an expert by actively tweeting valuable content yourself as well as searching for tweets in your particular field and replying to questions that are tweeted. Make sure to include your Twitter handle whenever you are at conferences or interact with any kind of media outlets. When it comes to the content of your tweets, remember that you are extremely limited in how much you can say on Twitter (140 characters), so keep your comments short, pithy—and authentic. Informality and immediacy are Twitter's hallmarks, and your tweets should represent you, your personality, and your interests.

Online Tool 4: Content Creation and Commentary

On the Internet, content is king, and the ability to create and post content in the form of articles, blog posts, teleseminars, webinars, slide decks of presentations, videos, audios, and so on, will position you as a contributor and potential leader in your field. In the funding and venture capital world, having an active online presence through blogs, content creation, and education is becoming a key marketplace advantage.

Prominent old-school VC firms like First Round Capital, Sequoia Capital, and Andreessen Horowitz have sites where they publish content about the industry, and industry insiders like Kay Koplovitz are blogging, tweeting, and reposting their content on LinkedIn and other sites. You, too, can increase your reach and impact and draw more connections to you while deepening your relationships with the ones you have by creating valuable, shareable content, and then distributing it across multiple platforms.

Online Tool 5: Facebook

I confess, I'm not that active on Facebook, nor are many of my power circle members. However, if you are a retailer or a service provider, or if you own a small business, Facebook is a key way for you to connect with and build an online community, all without "leaving the store," so to speak. There are three ways that power connectors use Facebook effectively.

First, it is a means for keeping in touch with your personal contacts and for sharing hobbies, life events, and so on. Facebook is a far more "social" social media platform where you can share things that might not quite fit on LinkedIn. (Your LinkedIn profile needs to be professional in tone and information; your business contacts may not want to see cute pictures of your kids or pets.)

Second, many people use Facebook to locate long-lost college room-mates or friends, or to reach out to people they may wish to know. Like LinkedIn, Facebook will recommend people who are connections of your connections, and you may discover a link to the individual you are looking to reach.

Third, depending on your business and/or network, your professional or business Facebook page is key—as long as you use it to actively engage with your customers or clients. Go on your page every day. Comment on posts, and reply to your customers' comments. Acknowledge compliments, and address complaints. Share valuable content or resources. Facebook allows its users to promote posts, and some small business owners have found this to be a useful tool for finding new customers and/or connections.

You also can Like the Facebook pages of others you wish to know. Many prominent figures have professional or fan pages, and by linking them, you can follow the content they post, comment on it, and share it with your net-work. Facebook is yet another way to stay engaged with people you know and to connect and add value to people you wish to know.

With all of these ways to connect online, and with many more certain to arise in the next few years, power connectors must keep abreast of social media trends and utilize them appropriately, depending upon their pro-fessional communities and goals. Social media stylist Jennifer Abernethy says, "Keep track of where eyeballs are going, what sites people are talking about. A year or so ago no one had heard of Instagram, and as of late 2013 it had 150 million users. Don't say things like, 'That's not for me—what do I need with a photo-sharing site?' These new platforms can expand your reach dramatically and lead to connections you couldn't make any other way."

However, I believe that for creating memorable relationships, nothing takes the place of face-to-face contact. And it's at conferences and meetings where we tend to encounter the greatest number of "important strangers" in person. Just as there are strategies for successfully building an online presence, there are secrets for making the most of conferences and meetings—as well as gaining entry to exclusive, high-level groups.

Using Conferences and Meetings for Power Connecting

It's all about personal contact. No matter how heavy your
workload is, do not allow yourself to work in your cubicle or
office all day, every day—for your own well-being and the
health of your business, you need to get out and about,
meeting people and developing relationships.

—RICHARD BRANSON

Not long ago at a conference in Miami, I gave a speech in which I talked
about networking. A man stood up and asked, "I'm an entrepreneur and just
starting out—how would I find someone to invest in my business?" I looked
at the rest of the audience and said, "Raise your hand if you're looking for
money." About half of the people in the room raised their hands. Then I said,
"Raise your hand if you're an individual on a VC board or you are an accred-
ited angel investor." A third of the people in the room raised their hands.
"There's your answer," I told the gentleman. "In any conference, meeting, or
group of 10 or more people, the solution to any problem is in the room."

Conferences are excellent places to meet new people in specific ecosystems. There are organizations for every ecosystem, interest, profession, and
field. For each of these organizations there are thought leaders and prominent
individuals, and often the best places to meet them face-to-face are at meetings and conferences at the local, state, regional, and national levels. However, just as you approach building your power circles strategically, you must
be strategic in (1) the conferences you choose to attend, (2) how you prepare
before your arrival, (3) what you do while there, and (4) how you follow up
afterward.

Choosing the Right Conferences

My friend Jeff is a telecommunications engineer who works as an independent consultant. His business is 100 percent referral based, and he is eager to
gain more clients. When we talked about his conference activity, he said that
he had been on panels and had given several speeches, but his efforts weren't
producing new business because he was speaking to other engineers! "Most
of the people in my network are just like me, and I don't know how to break

into other circles or get to the 'right folks,'" he complained. He said that most of his clients were business managers of midtier telecommunications companies.

"Do you know the conferences that kind of person attends?" I asked. He didn't, so I suggested that he start by attending the next meeting in his area of the Association for Corporate Growth, an organization dedicated to bringing midmarket business professionals together. "Talk with the chapter president," I said. "Ask who else in the room is in your industry. Find your competitors and vendors, and ask them which industry conferences and meetings you need to attend."

No one has enough time to attend all the conferences that might be beneficial to their career or network. That's why it's important to find the conferences that will provide the greatest opportunity for you to learn, grow, and connect with others at your level *or higher*. As one of my mentors once told me, "Don't attend a meeting if there isn't anybody smarter in the room than you or if there isn't anyone who can help you or whom you can help with your connections and expertise."

It's all about getting into the right room for your interests and goals. Do your research about past conference speakers and attendees. Is this conference populated by the top people in your industry? For example, the annual BIO-Europe conference is the largest life sciences meeting in the world. It's said that more deals are made in the halls and over coffee and meals there than are made in an entire year for some companies. If you want to access greater resources and opportunities, it's always a question of meeting the right people—and that happens when you're in the right room.

It's easy to get stuck in your own particular industry "silo," however, and miss conferences and meetings that could allow you access to key ecosystems. Make sure you cross-pollinate by also attending events that draw a wide variety of people. Go to TEDx events and other conferences about ideas as well as business. Attend community events and meetings where you can encounter people from political, media, and community ecosystems. (Remember my banker friend who joined the symphony to network with high-net-worth individuals in his city, or my time with United Way, where I got to know many of the top corporate executives from Idaho?) Join the groups where the people you wish to know congregate. Be selective, but be active; go to meetings regularly, volunteer for high-level projects, and take a position on the group's board of directors. If the group has local, state, regional, and national levels, attend the higher-level meetings when possible. And when you find the conferences and meetings that are the "right rooms" for you, attend them year after year so you become part of the conference ecosystem and, perhaps, one of its organizers.

Preparing to Attend

Your goal should be to maximize your time at any meeting or conference, and that means being prepared. First, make sure you have clear objectives and specific goals for attending. Do you want to acquire new connections? Meet key players? Solidify relationships with current contacts? How will you use this conference to increase and deepen your network?

Second, if it will be your first time at a particular conference, contact past attendees and ask them for any suggestions about how to get the most from your time there. You also may ask them if there are particular individuals they would suggest that you meet. Jaime Tardy, who has met and interviewed over 100 millionaires, suggests reaching out to key influencers to initiate a relationship before you attend. That way, you will have a ready-made and influential connection when you walk into the meeting.[9]

Third, get a list of all the speakers and decide which ones you wish to meet. Think of some questions you might ask, either during the Q&A sessions following their speeches or afterward. Prepare your introduction; review the share you created in Chapter 7, so you can be very clear and engaged when you talk about your business. Make sure your introduction also adds value and creates intrigue. (I met top investor Esther Dyson at a conference with a 30-second introduction.)

Fourth, see if you can get a list of all the people scheduled to attend the conference. Some organizations will send out a list in advance with information on each attendee (company, city they live in, and so on). Check the LinkedIn profiles of anyone whom you might be interested in meeting. You also might want to reach out to some attendees in advance. Consider this first contact an introduction of sorts, so personalize it to the individual, and include information about yourself, the reason you feel it would be good to meet, and a suggested time and place ("Let's meet at 8 a.m. Saturday morning in the restaurant"). You might put their LinkedIn profile photos in your smartphone—a very simple way to identify key players on site.

Fifth, utilize your social media before you go to the conference. Tweet or post your plans to attend on your own pages and Twitter feed. Many conferences today have Twitter hashtags set up, and speakers will post tweets to engage attendees' interest before the conference begins. Start commenting on the tweets and tweet yourself; it will get your name in front of the speakers and other conference attendees.

Sixth, bring business cards, of course, but also prepare to use social media while you are at the meeting or conference. Make sure your LinkedIn name and Twitter handle are on your cards. LinkedIn expert Wayne Breitbarth also suggests that you include in your LinkedIn profile links to helpful resources: "Then when you meet people at an event, you can suggest they go to your profile and look at or download materials that will help them. You'll be immediately adding value to a new relationship."[10]

Making the Most of Your Conference Time

As David Bradford, executive chair of HireVue, says, "Ninety percent of success in life comes from showing up. You have to be there to create the magic." Attending conferences gives you the opportunity for face-to-face meetings where you can build connections quickly with people you might not easily access otherwise. Some of the greatest advantages of conferences are the serendipitous meetings that occur when diverse people gather together. However, you have a relatively short time in which to initiate those conversations and establish those relationships. Here are 11 keys for maximizing your conference power connecting.

1. Arrive early. The 20 or 30 minutes before the sessions begin are prime opportunities to look for the people you wish to meet. Furthermore, arriving early will leave you time for chance encounters with others you may need to know. Arriving early for a particular speaker's session also makes it more likely you can get a front-row seat (a great position for asking a question or approaching the speaker after his or her talk).

2. Don't spend much time with people you already know. Unless one of your goals for the conference is to deepen your relationships with certain individuals, it's better to avoid hanging out with your "usual crowd" if they are at the event. Two Columbia professors once did a study of MBA students who attended after-work mixers with the stated goal of building their networks. They found that individuals tended to gravitate to people who were most like themselves. If they came to the mixer with friends, the friends would introduce them to their acquaintances, and the result was fewer encounters with strangers who might have been valuable weak link additions to their networks.[11] If you know many people at the conference, set up specific times to see them, but do your best to go off on your own and seek out those who may have different life experiences and backgrounds.

3. Strike up conversations with strangers. Remember, your goal isn't just to attend the conference but to connect with people who can benefit you and whom you can benefit. You can start by finding and introducing yourself to the people you contacted before the conference, but eventually you will have to speak with people you do not know. Every stranger is potentially valuable to you, so you must leave any shyness at home and be willing to approach complete strangers. It's easy to ask someone's opinion of a past or upcoming session ("Have you heard John Smith speak before?"), or to make a comment about the company or city listed on a name tag ("You come from Pittsburgh? My aunt lived there for many years"), or to ask a logistical question ("Do you know where I can get a good cup of coffee?"). Any of these questions can open up a conversation that may lead to a solid connection.

4. Identify and meet the connectors. There are power connectors at every conference; you just need to find them. An effective strategy is to ask a number of people, "Who do you know here?" If one name pops up frequently, he or she is usually a connector. You also can watch as people arrive and see if there is anyone that most of them greet—that's the person you want to meet too. Often some of the best-connected and knowledgeable people at the conference are the organizer and the volunteers. These are the people who do all the work and get very little of the credit. Find and introduce yourself to the conference organizer and/or host. Take the time to acknowledge the volunteers. A sincere compliment can help you establish valuable relationships.

5. Go where people congregate. Meeting new people is a combination of luck and synchronicity, but you can make yourself "luckier" by positioning yourself where they gather. David Bradford is a master connector, and one of his tips is, "Stand in high-traffic areas where you can be seen and heard." At conferences, that often means by the coffee or other food service areas. Other good places to meet people include by the registration tables and by the doorways of conference sessions—anywhere people are waiting.

6. Before sessions, look around you—whom can you meet? Every conference is full of big and small sessions that you may wish to attend. But you should still use these sessions as opportunities to make new connections. If you take your seat even a few minutes before the speaker goes on, use the time to meet and chat with the people seated beside, in front, and behind you. It's a great chance to make a quick connection that you can pursue later if you desire.

7. Have a plan for connecting with speakers. I mentioned earlier that you should have at least a couple of questions ready in case the speaker opens the floor for Q&As. But whether you ask a question or not, be ready to take advantage of the opportunity to approach the speaker either before or after the presentation. Remember that you will probably be one of a number of people who will be vying for the speaker's attention, so your introduction should be short, sweet, value adding, and intriguing. If the speaker is on Twitter, send a tweet to your network mentioning the session and including the speaker's hashtag. It's a simple way of following up immediately and keeping your name in front of him or her.

8. Choose your moment carefully. When seeking to connect with people, choose your moment. If they're standing alone, walk up and introduce yourself. If they're on the phone, texting, or checking e-mail, or if they are in conversation with other people, you can get close enough so they can see you, but give them a moment to finish the conversation, call, or e-mail before you speak or approach. Always check to see whether it is a good time or if they want you to come back later.

9. Introduce yourself successfully. At some conferences it can feel like everyone is a hungry barracuda searching out the best "fish" with whom to connect. A successful introduction at a conference is not a "Give-me-your-card-what's-your-LinkedIn-great-let's-keep-in-touch-next!" exchange. Instead, as I described in Chapter 7, it is an encounter where you connect and engage with other people, getting to know about what's important to them, adding value, and sharing about yourself. It's the first step that may lead to a request to follow up afterward.

10. Help others out by making beneficial introductions on the spot. I meet a lot of people at events, and if in the course of the conference I meet someone who is a good fit for someone else who is attending the conference, I'll say, "Let me grab so-and-so and introduce you." It's much easier for people to meet when there is someone to provide an introduction. It creates more connection and a stronger foundation for the relationship. This kind of introduction is another form of triangulation, and it benefits all parties concerned.

11. Get and give follow-up information whenever you end a conversation. See Chapter 7 for how to capture people's contact information. And remember, it's critical to follow up each new connection within 24 hours. At the end of each day of a conference, I will go through my notes and send LinkedIn requests and follow-up e-mails that add value to each person. Throughout the day I also will tweet about the conference and the people I meet, so that right from the start I am top of mind.

Following Up After the Conference Ends

As soon as possible, assess these new connections based on the system outlined in Chapter 8, and decide what your next steps should be to develop the relationships. Make sure you add them to your relationship chart and contact files. If they are on LinkedIn, see what groups, connections, and interests they list on their profile page. Check what kind of presence they have on social media; subscribe to their Twitter feeds and newsletters, read their blogs, and comment on the content they post online.

If there were people you wanted to meet but didn't have the opportunity while at the conference, you should reach out to them as quickly as possible afterward. Use the attendee list, or find them on LinkedIn and send a request noting that you were both at the same conference. Make sure that the invitation is warm and personal: refer to something that you shared at the conference, and let them know you wish to keep in touch.

Spiraling Up: Accessing More Exclusive Groups

Almost every charitable organization has an "inner circle" of donors who contribute the most, and every profession has an equivalent to that inner circle that is accessible to those with power, status, wealth—or connections. I'm seeing more and more "curated" private gatherings, where a top-level businessperson holds a dinner for a select group that includes clients, others who are potential clients or who could bring in clients, and those who are in charge of clients for the firm. In a more informal setting, it's easier for people to connect and build personal relationships that then carry over into business. You know you have a powerful network when you start to receive invitations to high-level private events like these.

Such conferences and meetings include industry meetings, community galas, art shows, theater previews, and so on. They are small (often 50 to 100 people or fewer), invitation-only events that bring together the movers and shakers in their respective ecosystems. When you are invited, you can pretty much guarantee that you will make some valuable connections there. Your attendance will not only give you a chance to meet and interact with influencers, but it will also increase both your credibility and reputation in their eyes.

Getting invited to such gatherings is a process of building trust, expressing interest, and proving to your connections in these groups that you can play at that level. If you're invited into a room of 50 people, all of whom are CEOs or top influencers in their ecosystems, you'll need to be able to speak their language and talk about their concerns as an equal. It can be unnerving—the first time I walked into such a group, I felt out of place. Just remember, however, that everyone is a human being with a set of problems, and you might have the exact knowledge, connection, resource, or opportunity that will solve a particular problem for someone in the room.

The people you know may get you invited to these exclusive groups, but it is who you *are* and what you can contribute that will get you invited back. Therefore, it's important that you enter these groups carefully, communicate with members appropriately, and add value intelligently—before, during, and after. At various Alley to the Valley conferences, I've met venture capitalist Heidi Roizen, *Shark Tank* investor Barbara Corcoran, and U.S. Treasurer Rosie Rios, and I was blown away by the fact that I was in the same room with these powerful women. But I also figured that I had resources at my disposal that might be of use. In high-level groups, adding value is the price of admission.

For power connectors, reaching out to people and spending time with them—one-on-one, in groups, at conferences, or on social media—is what builds strong, healthy, strategic networks. Interactive game producer Joseph Gonzalez reminds us, "Building a strong network of quality people is a powerful force multiplier that can pay huge dividends if intelligently utilized."

Connected Women: Building Success One Relationship at a Time

Put a networking woman into any room, anywhere, anytime, and
before you know it, opportunities for work, service, assistance,
employment, investment, and a new cleaning service blossom
like seeds do in time-lapse photography.

—VICTORIA PYNCHON

Many people will tell you that business today is more gender blind
than ever, and compared to 30 years ago, women have come
a long way, baby. My friend Kay Koplovitz (who was the first
female CEO of a television network) tells a story of being invited to the
media luncheon for the Masters Golf Tournament at Augusta National Golf
Club in Georgia in 1982.

The tournament chairman, Hord Hardin, escorted Kay and a dozen executives of other TV networks up the clubhouse stairs to the men's grill—only
to turn around, a concerned look on his face, and tell Kay, "Uh, we've got a
problem. We don't allow women on the second floor."

Undaunted, Kay said, "Well, Hord, what are we going to do about that?"

After only a moment's hesitation, Hord offered, "Well, I guess we'll eat
downstairs in the Trophy Room."[1]

I *thought* we had come a long way until I read that, years later, when Sheryl Sandberg was in a negotiation and asked for the restroom, the man across the table, who had been with the company for a year, was stumped. "Am I the only woman to have pitched a deal here in an entire year?" she asked. "I think so," he said, "or maybe you're the only one who had to use the bathroom."[2] No one will say that business today is gender *neutral*. How can it be, when there still are far fewer women than men in the upper echelons of business? According to Catalyst (a nonprofit organization that researches women and business), in 2013 in the United States women constituted 46.9 percent of the labor force. However, by the time women move from the entry level to the managerial level, that percentage drops to 37 percent. The higher you go up the corporate ladder, the fewer women you'll find: 26 percent of vice presidents and executives, 14.3 percent of executive committee members, and 4.2 percent of CEOs. Women hold only 16.6 percent of board seats, and they constitute only 8.1 percent of top earners.[3]

Those numbers are distressing, not just because the potential of half the population isn't being realized but also because there are clear *financial* benefits to having women in our corporations. A 2011 study showed that companies with more women in key management roles demonstrated an average 1 percent improvement in performance, representing more than $42 million in additional revenue yearly.[4] That same year, Catalyst also reported that companies whose board memberships were 19 to 44 percent female produced 26 percent greater returns on invested capital than companies with no women on their boards.[5] It's clear that business needs more women in positions of power—but to get there, women need to enhance their power connecting skills.

I rarely think of the process of building strategic relationships as being either masculine or feminine. After all, if everything you need is attached to other people, do you really care what gender they are as long as they can provide a solution to your problems? The fundamentals of connecting and adding value are the same for both sexes. However, there are some things men and women do differently, and if we ignore these differences, we run the risk of failing to create the kinds of strong business relationships we all desire. I'd like to offer a few suggestions that will hopefully help more women to acquire a seat in the boardroom or a suite on the C-level floor.

The Truth About Men and Women...

Men and women belong to different species, and communication
between them is still in its infancy.
—BILL COSBY

When I came of age in Idaho, most women didn't really question the fact that
men were running things and that most business networking happened on
the golf course or in men-only clubs.[6] However, I was fortunate enough to
be part of a generation that saw those conditions changing, albeit slowly. As I
progressed through the ranks of business and established great relationships in
the local and national financial, political, media, and community ecosystems,
I observed some key differences in the ways that men and women, in general,
develop their strategic networks. (Some of these observations may seem like
gender-biased stereotyping, but each is backed up with both research and
personal experience.)

Men build alliances. Women develop networks of relationships. When
men network, it's with the specific goal of building alliances that create
greater benefit for their members. "Men share resources *within* their network," points out Annette McClellan, "while women share resources as a
means for *expanding* their network." Women tend to reach out to broader
coalitions, they develop extensive interconnections with groups, and they
are more open to helping others both within and outside of those groups.
"We're wired to connect and form alliances, to cooperate and collaborate, and to support each other," says CEO of the All Access Group Kelli
Richards. This gives women an advantage of building more diverse networks
(see below), but they may find it harder to see their networks as entities they
can use for personal gain.

**Men network up and down. Women tend to network more peer to
peer.** The "old boys' network" plugs men into a vertically integrated
system, where senior people are expected to bring the next generation
along, and the next generation learns that those senior to them will happily be their mentors and sponsors. However, while women are becoming
better at reaching down to help other women up (see below), they tend

to network horizontally, peer to peer, rather than seeking out higher-level individuals who have the greater knowledge, skill, and connections they need. Worse yet, because there are fewer women in the upper echelons of business, the size of the "old girls' network" is still very small and thus, harder to access.

Men are rewarded for "taking charge." Women are rewarded for "taking care." In 2007, a report by Catalyst outlined a fundamental dilemma for women in business: the "taking charge" behaviors (assertiveness, authoritativeness, and dominance) are more associated with effective leadership, while the "taking care" behaviors associated with women (helping, nurturing, and being likable) make them seem soft and less capable of leading others. "When women act in ways that are consistent with gender stereotypes, they are viewed as less competent leaders (too soft)," the report states. "When women act in ways that are inconsistent with such stereotypes, they're considered as unfeminine (too tough)."[7] Women are caught in a "damned if they do, doomed if they don't" dilemma that marketing and branding consultant Dorie Clark knows all too well. "The nicer and warmer you're perceived to be, the dumber your colleagues often think you are—but you don't want to overcompensate and act like a jerk," she says.

The irony is that the "take care" behaviors of women are much better for creating strong connections and building relationships in business. For example, women use more emotional intelligence to be aware of the needs of others. They add value by focusing on the little things that make people feel special, like remembering a birthday, sending an article of interest, or sharing information about a great new restaurant. Women are better at communicating consistently and adding a personal touch to communication. Because women are seen as having greater empathy and focus on others, even as they climb the corporate ladder, they often maintain greater likability at every stage, whereas male leaders tend to be viewed more negatively the higher they go.[8] To be successful, women must combine "taking charge" strengths with "taking care" connections.

Men create teams. Women collaborate. The older model of teamwork in business was to pull together a group to focus on a particular task. One person was in charge, and each person on the team had certain responsibilities. While you relied on your teammates to get their jobs done, you partnered with them more from necessity than preference.

Today, however, business is more about collaboration and assembling diverse, multidisciplinary groups to work together toward a common goal. There is greater emphasis on building trust, cooperation, longer-lasting relationships between people, and greater inclusion—a mix that produces a wider variety of opinions and more creative solutions. Collaborative, relationship-based leadership is becoming more of the norm, and it is a norm that plays to women's strengths.

In 2012, researchers John Gerzema and Michael D'Antonio asked 64,000 businesspeople around the world to classify 125 human qualities, either by gender or by which traits were most important to leadership, success, and happiness. Their research results showed that the attributes considered most relevant for leadership today—collaboration, transparency, inclusion, mentoring, and innovation—were most frequently associated with women.[9] "If Lehman Brothers had been Lehman Brothers and Sisters, we probably wouldn't have had our financial meltdown," comments Betty Spence, president of the National Association of Female Executives.

Men are rewarded for advocating for themselves. Women are rewarded for advocating for others. The ask can be hard for all of us to make, but women seem to have a harder time of it. Again, cultural expectations come into play: it's expected that men will promote themselves, assert their qualifications, and negotiate to get the best deal possible for themselves. However, women are expected to be "other oriented and caring," writes Adam Grant, citing research done by economist Linda Babcock and colleagues. If women promote themselves and ask for what they want, they are seen as selfish and "not team players."[10]

Research by influence expert Robert Cialdini shows that women who are perceived as boasting about their accomplishments run the risk of harming their status interpersonally.[11] All of this makes it more difficult for women to be effective advocates for themselves. However, when women advocate for *others*, they fare better. Babcock and her colleagues asked 176 senior executives to play the role of an employee who was being promoted and needed to negotiate a new salary. The male executives negotiated an average compensation of $146,000, where the women averaged $141,000—3 percent less. However, when Babcock asked the female executives to imagine they were mentors negotiating on the employee's behalf (that is, advocating for someone else), the women produced an average compensation of $167,000.[12] Whether it's because women are more effective asking for a benefit for someone else or because their audience is more receptive to an "other oriented" request, advocating for others seems to be a winning strategy for women.

Men are sponsored. Women are mentored. According to a 2012 Catalyst study, 47 percent of high-potential women in corporations around the world are assigned a mentor, compared to 39 percent of men. However, "having more *mentors* didn't lead to advancement; rather, having senior mentors who are in a position to provide *sponsorship* did"[13] (italics mine). Mentors show you the ropes and give feedback and advice on your work, job, profession, or career. They serve as caring yet impartial sounding boards and guides to help you navigate the complexities of business. Sponsors, on the other hand, are highly placed enough to be able to use their influence to secure your advancement.

A sponsor's goal is not just to advise and guide but also to advocate and actively promote. And considering that women (1) have difficulty advocating for themselves and (2) are seen negatively if they pursue advancement too aggressively, it's clear why having a sponsor—someone in a position of power speak on their behalf—would be extremely beneficial.

Men trade favors. Women help. Men excel at transactional relationships: "I'll help you, and at some point I'll call in the favor." (Adam Grant refers to this as "matching" behavior.) Women tend to give within the context of developing the greater relationship. If asked for help, they will usually provide it if they can, but without the quid pro quo of trading favors. They add value consistently, with the idea that by continuing to do so, they build a stronger, longer-lasting relationship that will make it more likely that you will help them when they need it. There are a couple of downsides to this relationship-based approach, however. First, with the expectation that women are naturally inclined to take care of and help others, the help they provide can be undervalued and underappreciated.

Second, as founder and CEO of the Thought Leadership Lab Denise Brosseau states, "Women don't always understand the give-and-take of business relationships—they are frequently good at giving freely but don't always ask for the help they need." As you remember from Chapter 8, professional relationships are based on value added and *received*. Women need to be willing not just to be the givers but also to allow the others in their networks to provide value when they need it.

Men network with those who are like themselves. Women do too—but they're better at diversity. VC investor Whitney Johnson observes, "Men tend to introduce men to men and women to women, so we get stuck in the girls' club." Certainly, it's natural for people to be drawn to others who are like them and to choose to build networks from individuals who share their backgrounds, values, habits, and so on. But as I said in Chapter 4, homogenous networks don't provide the kind of diversity needed for success.

The good news is that, as Sharon Hadary, coauthor of *How Women Lead,* writes, "Women are more likely to bring together people from different backgrounds, perhaps from different parts of the company, or different parts of their lives."[14] Women tend to be more eclectic in their connections, and they recognize the value represented even by what can seem like an inconsequential relationship. A dry cleaner or hairdresser may introduce you to the investor you need for your business; the son of a friend may lead you to your next great product. The kinds of horizontal networks women build give them a broad reach and allow them to create more powerfully diverse networks by bridging ecosystems, localities, and generations.

Those are not hard-and-fast rules; I've known many women who exhibit great take-charge leadership qualities and men who are excellent at collaboration and connection. The point I wish to make is that both men and women have strengths that they should borrow from one another appropriately, depending on the needs of the situation. More important, I believe that *all* of us, men and women, should prioritize the attitudes and behaviors that will help us build and maintain strong relationships.

Power Connecting Strategies for Women

> We can't build successful careers we love alone or in a
> vacuum.... We need great supporters, ambassadors, and
> partners who believe in us 100 percent and can help us
> elevate and launch to the next level.
>
> —KATHY CAPRINO

Most women are born connectors, and many of the power connecting strategies in this book—adding value, empathizing, creating relationships, and so on—will seem natural. However, other skills—like creating a powerful ask, seeking out strategic relationships, excluding people from power circles—are less so. To become true *power* connectors, women should add the following to their current networking endeavors.

Strategically connect—up, down, and sideways. Too many entrepreneurial women have not had access to guidance from successful entrepreneurs who can show them the way to succeed. They need to actively seek out and build strong relationships with individuals they believe will be of assistance to them in their careers and businesses. In particular, they need to network "up," putting themselves in front of those who can be their formal or informal sponsors and advocate for them in executive committees, boardrooms, and business communities.

Kay Koplovitz (who's sponsored and mentored many women through Springboard) suggests that women establish relationships with people they admire in their companies or industries. If they don't have a way to reach them directly, she suggests that they look for ways to bridge the gap by adding value. "You can do this by offering up your assistance on a project, a task force, and an industrywide initiative, or by participating in a common interest—for example, on a health issue, a hobby, or a community event," Kay writes. "You might find that there are ways to exchange value, providing the mentor with information on something of interest to them. Creating this two-way street is the best way to develop a long-term relationship."[15]

While it's important to participate in all kinds of networks, women should seek to build strategic relationships with female peers. Women-only peer groups provide mutual support in a space that many women feel is more comfortable and where members understand one another. However, the goal of peer networks is not only mutual support but also mutual *expansion*—of points of view, spheres of influence, and ranges of experience. Therefore, women also should develop peer-to-peer networks that bring together diverse individuals from different ecosystems.

At the higher levels, this is happening already. As Pamela Ryckman points out in *Stiletto Network: Inside the Women's Power Circles That Are Changing the Face of Business*, "Many of the top women in technology now know the top women in finance, who know the top women in media, who know the top women in law, who know the top women in retail, and so on."[16] Women at every level should get to know their peers of all races, ethnicities, experiences, and industries; by reaching horizontally across conventional silos, they will enrich their connections and broaden their outlooks.

Finally, women need to pay it forward by reaching out to those who are just entering professional life. There's a great story about renowned attorney and judge Abner J. Mikva. While in his first year of law school, Mikva wanted to volunteer for the Democratic Party in Chicago. He went to the local party office, where he was asked, "Who sent you?" When Mikva replied, "Nobody," he was sent packing with the comment, "We don't want nobody nobody sent." After that, Mikva decided he wanted to become "a somebody who sent future somebodies," and in 2010 his protégée, Elena Kagan, became only the fourth female Supreme Court associate justice in history.[17] Women who have succeeded also need to connect with "future somebodies" by looking around, seeing who's coming up, and asking how they can help.

Speak up. Ask for what you want, and stand up for yourself—nicely. In 2012 researcher Athena Vongalis-Macrow did a study of the networking efforts of 74 middle management women in three organizations. More than 65 percent said that they believed networking had helped them in their careers, and they identified helping others, offering career advice, and supporting the career plans of others as key strategies. However, only 4 percent talked to others about their own work or career goals. "Part of the reasoning was that they did not want to appear too ambitious or boastful; some wanted to minimize disappointment or the appearance of failure if the goals were not achieved," writes Vongalis-Macrow.[18] But if these women didn't let people know what they wanted, how could others be of any help?

Asking for what you want is not something women are comfortable doing, as film producer Elizabeth Dell understands all too well. "I think it's easier for women to develop strategic relationships, but sometimes harder to use them," she says. "Developing strong relationships is something that's very naturally 'female'—keeping the group together, making sure interests are aligned, everyone is happy—but asking for resources for oneself, whether it's money or promotions or projects, is too tough or forward or aggressive. We do less well in making 'the ask' in a relationship." Women need to overcome any risk aversion they may be feeling and be courageous enough to speak up—declaring what they need and having the confidence to follow through. They must become experts at converting introductions and relationships into greater opportunities and business.

There are ways that women can bring some "caring" behavior to bear when showcasing their skills and accomplishments and proposing themselves for high-level positions. It's been shown that a combination of niceness and insistence (what University of Michigan president Mary Sue Coleman called being "relentlessly pleasant"[19]) can produce a more positive reaction when women speak up for themselves. My mother used to say, "You can catch more flies with honey than you can with vinegar," and I have always found that being both pleasant and firm usually leads to the desired result.

Asking for what you want may feel odd, but it is a more businesslike and professional approach. What's more important, as Kay Koplovitz points out, at the end of the day people treat you the way you treat yourself. Respecting yourself enough to ask for what you want shows others that they should respect you too.

Support other women. Gloria Vanderbilt once said, "I've always believed that one woman's success can only help another woman's success." Women need to make sure to include other women in their networks, building strategic relationships that allow for exchanges of value and mutual support. By doing this, women only make one another stronger, both personally and professionally.

Sometimes, however, it can be a challenge to find other women to support simply because there are fewer of them—and often they tend to put their heads down, get the work done, and never think to expand their circle of connections. When 30Second Mobile founder Elisa All and Springboard founder Amy Millman went to a recent meeting of the Chicago Founders Circle CEO networking group, for example, they were disappointed that there were only two other women in the room. After the meeting, Elisa All commented, "I would love to see women lean on each other more, support each other in the workplace and business to business, and invest in each other. This will help get us where we need to be." Women need to make building their power circles of strategic relationships with women in diverse ecosystems as high a priority as doing well in their careers.

Women also need to promote the efforts of other women by offering to open doors for them. There are two sets of words we need to use constantly. The first is, "How can I help?" And the second is equally powerful: "Use my name." "If anyone could grant me one wish, it would be for all women everywhere to say these three words along with another woman's name at least once a week," writes *Forbes* contributor Victoria Pynchon.[20] With those two phrases, women can open the right doors for other women by turning cold calls into warm introductions.

The good news is that when you become a power connector, your name has great power. If someone calls or e-mails me and says, "Kay Koplovitz said we should talk," you'd better believe that I get on the phone. And when I tell a connection to reach out to so-and-so and to say, "Judy sent me," I'm certain that my name will open the door. I believe that women have an obligation to offer that kind of support to other women. As Gail Blanke, CEO of Lifedesigns, says, "Don't just stand for the success of other women. Insist on it." We still have to use our common sense and discernment—after all, with each introduction we put our reputations on the line—but we should be generous with favors and always thinking of whom our female colleagues need to know.

Ultimately, women may find they are assembling their own versions of what Pamela Ryckman calls a "stiletto network": women who actively support one another in achieving their goals. Such networks occur when women use the skills of power connecting to benefit one another.

I've had the privilege of being part of many such groups and benefiting from the relationships that are nurtured in the meeting of women with common minds, skills, goals, and experiences. Based on what I've seen, I believe that women provide a model of what's possible when power connecting is done the right way because we apply our natural caring skills—collaborating, adding value, bringing together diverse individuals, empathy, inclusion, and mentoring—to our professional relationships. It's clear that, in business as in life, women are better off (power) connected than we are apart.

Power Connections Are Connections First

One fundamental "rule" of the power game never becomes
outdated: the importance of treating people with respect
and courtesy. Always connect.

—ROBERT DILENSCHNEIDER

Not long ago someone close to me had a serious health problem. It was a journey of many doctors, treatments, even cities ... a journey that ended happily, thank goodness. But during the course of those months, the importance of being connected to great people became abundantly clear. I knew that I could rely on any of my power circle members to point me in the direction of the best resources available, to call and send supportive e-mails, and mostly to tell me, "You're not alone."

It proved to me again what I have always known: prosperity, fulfillment, and happiness arise through the people we know and the connections we make. Succeeding in business and in life is all about making connections. Every time more people are connected—with a book, on a plane, through the Internet—the GDP of the world goes up. "There is tremendous power in connecting with people," interactive game producer Joseph Gonzalez says. "Through connections you can create synergies of resources, knowledge, and capabilities. You never know who you're going to meet or how you might be able to help each other." The more connections, the more creativity, the more outreach, the more understanding, the more synergy—and the better the world becomes.

It's also pretty clear that the world as a whole is moving in the "direction of connection." We can connect online and develop friendships with people whom we may never meet in the flesh. We can call and Skype and FaceTime and Google Chat and Hangout with friends or contacts on the other side of the world. This ability to connect with anyone, anywhere has upended traditional business practices. "What we're seeing now is literally a shift in the way that people do business—a shift from hierarchical architectures to networked architectures," says Fred Wilson, a leading venture capitalist.[1]

Business is more relationship based than ever, and the value of our connections has never been higher. Your connections can matter more than your background, location, age, appearance, gender, or social status. No matter what their backgrounds are or where they come from, people who have a wealth of quality connections can access the kinds of opportunities and resources that lead to greater success. "Finding and building a network will be more valuable to you than an MBA," asserts Dale Stephens, author of *Hacking Your Education*.[2]

However, this new "age of connection" is *not* transactional. Today people are looking to develop relationships that are far more than just commercial exchanges. They want to spend their time and energy with others who they feel will be there for them when they need it, and vice versa. As InfusionSoft CEO Clate Mask says, "Sometimes when people engage in business relationships, it feels very much like two people trying to make money off of each other, and I don't find that enjoyable or satisfying. I'm not interested in developing business relationships; I want to create relationships on a deeper level." Such relationships are based on *multiplied emotional capital*: the value that each person contributes freely to the relationship multiplies the level of closeness and trust that both parties experience. It is that multiplication of value that is the hallmark of power connector relationships. In this final chapter I'd like to talk a little more about the fundamentals of power connection and the effects that relationships can have on ourselves, our businesses, our communities, and our world.

The Fundamentals of True Power Connections

Try not to become a man of success. Rather, try to become a
man of value.

—ALBERT EINSTEIN

If you had told me when I graduated from high school that today I would be connected to some of the most powerful people on earth, I would have thought you were crazy. I wasn't born in the right place, I don't have the right degrees, I'm a woman, I was raised Mormon, I didn't go to Harvard. But I have discovered that none of that matters, as long as you understand (and adopt) the following attitudes and characteristics of a power connector.

Power connectors are true to themselves while bringing their best to every relationship. One of the greatest pleasures of my life is to teach others to be power connectors. I've taken people who have never tried to network or to build business relationships and, with a little guidance and coaching, watched them blossom as they discovered the excitement of creating great relationships. And the best part, to me, is that all they had to do was to overcome their fears and simply be themselves.

To connect, I believe that you must be authentically true to yourself and who you are. But power connectors take this one step further, with a commitment to be at their *best* in each relationship. Like attracts like, remember; and power connectors understand that in order to attract the highest caliber people to their networks, they must be high caliber themselves. Power connectors will settle for nothing less than bringing only the best of who they are to every relationship.

Power connectors genuinely care for and want to help others. One of my favorite quotes is by John Andrew Holmes: "It is well to remember that the entire universe, with one trifling exception, is composed of others." Power connectors understand that they must genuinely focus on other people so that they may discover their goals, needs, and desires, and to do whatever they can to help. I believe that caring for others is part of a power connector's DNA.

An example of this drive to help others is the founder of Who@, Lee Blaylock. Lee speaks with more than a hundred entrepreneurs and "wantra-preneurs" each month, and he actively mentors start-ups because, he says, "I genuinely like to help other people. It's in my core nature and my Christian faith. Some of the greatest feelings I've ever had in business are when I give people advice and they take it and it changes the vector of their business and makes them happy." Lee is an example of the "give first, and give often" attitude of a true power connector.

Power connectors are open to, and actively seek out, relationships with strangers. According to a 2008 study of social fears and phobias, 16.8 percent of adults in the United States fear meeting new people, and 13.1 percent are afraid of talking with strangers.[3] However, power connectors believe that every stranger represents a potentially valuable new connection. Therefore, they make it a point to reach out to people they do not know—usually by either (1) utilizing someone in their current networks to provide an introduction or (2) finding a way to add value immediately, often with the initial contact. (Remember, the value provided can be in the form of information, resources, opportunities, or connections.)

Power connectors also pay attention whenever someone they do not know contacts them. They recognize that every new contact may be the next big deal, the next vital link, or a new friend, so they are happy to explore new relationships. Power connectors believe, with the poet William Butler Yeats, that "there are no strangers here; only friends you haven't met yet."

Power connectors follow up and follow through. Power connectors believe in "response-ability"—meaning that they view it as an obligation to respond as soon as they are able. They know that great relationships are built through regular connection and absolute integrity. They are vigilant about responding to communications within 24 hours whenever possible. They keep in touch regularly with their power circle members (once every day or so with their Top 5, once a week with their Key 50, and once a month with their Vital 100). They reach out through multiple means—face-to-face meetings, phone, e-mail, social media—and they do their best to add personal touches that let people know they are top of mind. When someone provides them with an introduction, power connectors not only follow up immediately with the new contact but they also keep the introducer in the loop to let him or her know how the relationship is developing. Power connectors always follow through. They keep their commitments to others and regard their word as their bond.

Power connectors focus relentlessly on adding value—first, last, and always. Jay Allen, master networker and the president and cofounder of CXO, says, "Until you've given meaningful things a couple of times, you haven't established a relationship." Power connectors know that strong relationships are built on adding meaningful value to others. They add value in the first meeting, and they continue to add value throughout the relationship. They distinguish themselves by adding value (1) appropriately, (2) uniquely, (3) freely, (4) intelligently, and (5) consistently.

"Appropriate" value is based on the needs and goals of the other person, and it is delivered in such a way that he or she can receive it happily. Jay Allen is an expert in creating value through "warm" introductions. One time, he wished to help a client who wanted to do business with the Frontier Airlines CIO, so Jay called the CIO and asked for a meeting. During the course of the conversation, Jay asked the CIO how he could help. "I'm new in town and new to this position, so I'd really like to meet some of the CIOs of other airlines," the man said. So Jay cold-called the CIOs of both U.S. Airways and Northwest Airlines, and he got them to agree to meet with Frontier's CIO. It was exactly the value needed; and when Jay called again to ask if he would meet with his client, the CIO happily agreed.

The value added doesn't even have to be huge, but if it's added at the right place and time, it can completely transform someone's experience. The right introduction, at the right time, led to this book. The right enthusiastic phone call, at the right time, led to six years' worth of deals with Eileen Shapiro, the coauthor of *Make Your Own Luck*, and connecting with her coauthor and the father of the study of entrepreneurship, Howard Stevenson. Doing a favor for Stephanie Newby, the founder of the Golden Seeds Angel Network, by introducing her friend Jackie Zehner around town led to brunch with Gloria Steinem and Geena Davis, which led to my being able to help another friend get funding for her business after eight long years. None of these value-adds took much time, but because they were suited to the needs and goals of the individuals involved, they produced significant results.

Power connectors who are truly wise seek to add value based upon their unique gifts and strengths. Wharton professor Adam Grant, an expert on giving and the author of *Give and Take*, suggests this: "Figure out what kind of giving and helping you enjoy, and become uniquely good at that. You don't have to have a 'grab bag' of being helpful. Think of it more as, 'I do these things uniquely well, and it's fun for me.' If it's knowledge, share that; if you're passionate about making introductions, do that. If you take a lot of satisfaction in recognizing people whose work is invisible, write a thank-you note to the customer service person's boss."[4] I firmly believe that when we add value by sharing our gifts—whatever they may be—we make the world a better place.

Power connectors add value freely, without expectation of return or a quid pro quo. Yet they also add value intelligently—meaning (as Adam Grant says) that they are "otherish" givers who keep their own goals and needs in mind. Power connectors know the difference between saying, "My needs first," and, "My needs matter," so they add value in ways that leave them feeling satisfied rather than depleted. The goal for power connectors is to form authentic relationships with a sense of balanced give-and-take between all parties.

Finally, power connectors appreciate that adding value consistently is vital for establishing and maintaining good relationships. Great companies like Zappos and the Four Seasons know that consistently outstanding customer service that goes above and beyond creates strong relationships and raving fans. Great connectors like Adam Rifkin in Silicon Valley are equally consistent in adding value to others. When Rifkin first joined LinkedIn in 2003, he did three introductions each and every day. Over time, he had provided introductions and connections to over 10,000 people on LinkedIn.[5] With every gesture, every introduction, every piece of information or resource or opportunity provided, power connectors deepen their relationships with others.

Power connectors understand the greatest value they can add is connecting people with one another. In 2011 I had the pleasure of meeting Deborah Perry-Piscone, founder of Alley to the Valley. When another connection needed information about China, I asked Deborah, "Who do you know with experience in the Chinese market?"

She introduced me to Olin Wethington, who has worked for several presidents and has a vast network of connections in China. On a trip to New York, I took Olin to meet Joseph Koren, the founder of Daniel K. Jewelers. Joseph had mentioned to me that while Daniel K. had an enormous following in many countries, including Australia and Russia, the company had not been able to enter the Chinese market. I sugggested that Olin might be able to provide him with some valuable insights. (While we were in the store, Joseph let me hold a diamond that was later sold for tens of millions of dollars. One of the perks of connecting with the right people!)

Power connectors know that the biggest value they possess is represented by their connections and that the way to add the greatest value is often to connect people with one another. The people that you know and the connections you have built with them are your greatest wealth.

Power connectors ask appropriately, intelligently, and at the right time. When it comes time to ask for assistance or support, power connectors are confident that their connections will be excited to help and delighted that they can return one of the many favors they have received. However, power connectors are smart about whom they ask and when they make the request. While they know the answers or resources they need may come from unexpected sources (see below), they also recognize that asking the right people—based on their expertise and the ecosystems in which they operate—will go a long way toward determining the quality of the value their connections can provide. They ask investors and venture capitalists for access to funding, community leaders for help on the local level, artists for connections to other members of the creative world, and so on.

And they are sensitive about the timing of their requests as well. Because they stay connected with people consistently, they know not to ask for financing if the venture capitalist has just lost a lot of money on an investment, or to bother a new parent or someone who just changed jobs. If it's not the right time, power connectors either wait or, more likely, ask someone else in their power circles for help, knowing that the value provided through the years will almost certainly produce a positive response.

Whenever they ask, power connectors do their best to add more value at the same time. When this is done in groups, it's called an "ask and offer," "Jeffersonian dinner," or "reciprocity ring." The attendees talk about what they need or want and what they have to offer. I saw the power of this not long ago at an Alley to the Valley conference. There were only 50 people in the room, and we were divided into tables of four people each. We took turns discussing what we needed, and the others offered their help. Over the course of a day, millions were raised, book deals were put in motion, and board seats were filled. Adding value with an ask makes both giver and receiver feel good about the interaction.

When people do favors for power connectors, they always express their thanks and let the givers know the impact of the favors. I read recently about a woman who had tracked the impact of each introduction she had received from members of her network, and at Christmas she e-mailed 150 people to let them know how much they had done for her. Of those she e-mailed, 70 of them replied to her within 24 hours to let her know they were deeply touched by the gesture.[6]

Adam Grant suggests that letting people know their impact on your life is one of the best ways to say thank you to mentors, sponsors, or other movers and shakers. "Relationships are a two-way street, so you should never underestimate the value of the opportunity for someone else to be a giver," Grant says. "The best thing you can do is to help them see how much you appreciate them. Tell them how what they said affected you, or describe how you'll pay it forward."[7] Gratitude is an essential emotion for power connectors because they are very aware of how much they have received as well as how much they give.

Power connectors know the value they need may come from unexpected sources. Because they understand the principle of "what goes around comes around," power connectors know that the help they need may or may not come from the people to whom they've given the most. There's an old saying: "You have to shake the apple tree hard to get the apples to fall, but it's never the apple tree that you shake." The help that power connectors need often comes from unexpected places.

David Bradford, executive chair of HireVue, is a true power connector who is generous with his time and advice. Not long ago he met with an unemployed gentleman to see if he could help him with his job search. At the end of the meeting, the gentleman said, "Now, how can I help you?" David demurred, but the gentleman took him by the shoulders and insisted: "I'm asking you, *how can I help you?*" David had been trying to get funding for a client's business proposition, so he said, "You wouldn't know anyone who'd be interested in funding an international sports fund, would you?" The man thought for a minute and replied, "I know Prince So-and-So from Saudi Arabia. He has a home in Los Angeles—I'd be happy to introduce you." Within a few days David flew to Los Angeles to meet with the prince. Adding value without expecting a return led this power connector to the exact resource he needed.

Power connectors build trust over time. Power connectors understand that they must treat their relationships with the respect and attention they deserve, and they build trust by providing value appropriately, freely, intelligently, and consistently. They demonstrate both warmth and competence, and by doing so, they create strong mutual connections with others.

Power connectors believe that "to whom much is given, much is expected." They seek to uplift and help others. Janet Hanson is one of the founders of 85 Broads, and she is an incredibly successful power connector. She has spent almost two decades actively working to help others—in particular, young women—succeed by sharing her knowledge, resources, opportunities, and connections.

In 2005 she brought together 11 young women who were all interested in finance, and over the summer she taught them to go from being savvy consumers to savvy investors by showing them how to (1) identify companies with products they loved and (2) evaluate those companies as possible investments. A few years later one of those interns, Alexa von Tobel, launched LearnVest, an Internet-based financial planning company. "When somebody says, 'Well, what do you invest in?' I could say, 'I own stocks or bonds or mutual funds,' but what I really love to say is that I'm passionate about investing in other women,"[8] remarks Janet. "My greatest 'ROI on life' has been watching young entrepreneurs like Alexa brilliantly and fearlessly go for it, just like I did."[9]

Power connectors understand that the price of admission to the upper levels of connection is not simply giving to others but also giving back. They believe, as James Heller wrote, "A candle loses nothing by lighting another candle." And they are excited to see how they can add value to others that will help them become power connectors as well.

Power connectors know that who they become in the process of giving is more important than anything they may receive. Power connectors may enrich others when they add value, but I believe that they enrich themselves even more—by becoming the kind of people with whom others are eager to connect. Power connectors learn the importance of warmth, caring, and empathy combined with acuity, competence, and trustworthiness, and they embody those qualities completely. With a relentless focus on adding value, they embrace the identity of givers.

Power connectors come from a place of abundance because they know that whatever idea, information, resource, or opportunity someone needs, it is only a few connections away at most—and perhaps, it will be found in the hands of the next person they encounter. Most of all, power connectors feel that they are living at their best, doing exactly what they are meant to do.

As power connectors transform themselves by building connections based on warmth, competence, and contribution, they also transform the character and quality of the people with whom they are in relationships. By setting the tone of helping others, providing resources, warm connections, and "response-ability," they establish a common identity and standard for other group members.

As power connectors' connections help one another, they are contributing to the group's success and making each member better off. It becomes an upward spiral of connection, assistance, and augmented value that uplifts everyone. Events of a greater magnitude start happening closer together, and the successes of each member become the successes of the entire group, with positive impact spreading to all. This upward spiral transforms a network into something much closer and stronger, more vital and lasting. It transforms the network into a community.

Power connectors build communities of value. Just as billions of computers around the world become the Internet, and billions of individual cells form a human body, the people drawn together by a power connector form a distinct community with a life of its own. Communities possess resources that, in combination, have far more value than that which any individual can create, and that value can then be shared with the world at large.

Our communities have a greater reach than any one person, and their power for good or ill is immense. That's why I believe that power connectors have a responsibility to build communities based on both *sharing value* and *shared values*. Our power connector communities need to promote values like generosity, helpfulness, accomplishment, trust, responsibility, and caring.

We need to choose the members of our communities with care and then help them understand and embody the values that the community espouses— because each member has the power to take those values back to his or her own networks. If we are indeed within six degrees of separation from most of the people on the planet, then our power-connected communities can help to create a culture of connection in cities, ecosystems, families, businesses, and perhaps even countries. And that, I believe, is a power connector's rent for being on earth.

The Power of Connection

> Connections give purpose and meaning to our lives.
> —BRENÉ BROWN

Ultimately, I believe that success is not based on power connection but the power *of* connection. The strength of our relationships is what enables us to find everything we could ever want or need. And building, nurturing, and maintaining those relationships through ongoing attention and value is what turns us into better people who have the potential to create better communities and a better world.

This book is the product of such a power-connected community. It has been enriched and enlivened by the voices of the people in my power circles, individuals who were willing to take their time and share their stories and beliefs about the power of connection. I can think of no more fitting way to conclude this book than with the wise words of one of those people. Reginald (Reggie) Hughes served as CEO for hospitals in Alaska, Wyoming, and Utah, and then became CFO for a high-tech firm. Now he specializes in writing business plans that help companies raise investment capital, and helping them form business alliances. When I asked Reggie, "What advice would you give someone who wants to become a power connector?" this was his reply:

> *Be completely honest. Always own up to a mistake if you've made one. It's more important to be nice than to be right. Forget about your ego, and look out for the feelings and welfare of your business associates and clients. Go the "extra mile" and "toil upward through the night" when necessary. Trust that if you put others first and do an honest job, you will rise to the top somewhere along the way. Never criticize anyone. Never burn bridges. People change—cut them some slack and be forgiving. But if you encounter someone who is not worthy of your trust and respect, politely and quietly disassociate yourself.*
>
> *In the end, the most important thing will not be the titles you have held or the money you have made but the kind of person you have become.*

I believe you will find, as I have, that it is your connections that make your business and life truly abundant, wealthy, fulfilled, and successful. I wish you well as you create your own power-connected community.

Afterword

Top 10 Tips from the Titanium Rolodex

1. Start with the Three Golden Questions: "How can I help you?" "What ideas do you have for me?" "Who else do you know that I should talk to?"
2. If you're not succeeding, you're in the wrong room. Most people get stuck looking for love in all the wrong places.
3. For every tough problem, there is a match with the solution. Critical resources are attached to people.
4. Measure the value of your contacts not by their net worth but by whether they have a good head, heart, and gut.
5. Stranger danger is a fallacy. You're an adult.
6. People must know, like, and trust you before sharing valuable social capital.
7. Don't get lost in a crowd. Create a wide, deep, and robust network of your Key 50 that you carefully water, bathe in sunshine, and fertilize to grow—and that you prune as needed.
8. Keep the *rule of two*: give two favors before asking.
9. Introductions are your most valuable commodities, so only curate win-win connections: What is the value proposition for both parties?
10. If you can remember only one tip, make it this one: engage in random acts of kindness. You never know how one small act can tip the scales.

Notes

Chapter 1

1. Relational Capital Group, *A Better Way to Measure & Value Business Relationships: The Enterprise Relational Quotient™ Assessment*, white paper (Newtown Square, PA: Relational Capital Group, 2010), p. 3.
2. Ibid.
3. Adecco, *The Intrinsic Link Between Human and Relational Capital*, white paper, © 2007 Adecco, 877.8.adecco, adeccousa.com, Melville, NY, p. 2.
4. Gary Nielson, Ranjay Gulati, and David Kletter, *Organizing for Success in the Twenty-First Century: The Relationship-Centric Organization*, white paper (McLean, VA: Booz Allen Hamilton, 2002), p. 2.
5. Ronald S. Burt, *Brokerage and Closure: An Introduction to Social Capital* (New York: Oxford University Press, 2005), p. 3.
6. Daniel McGinn, "What VCs Really Care About," *Inc.* magazine, October 30, 2012, http://www.inc.com/magazine/201211/daniel-mcginn/what-vcs-really-care-about.html.
7. See Randall Collins, *The Sociology of Philosophies: A Global Theory of Intellectual Change* (Cambridge, MA: Belknap Press of Harvard University Press, 1998).

Chapter 2

1. As of 2011, Internet users had an average of 669 social ties each. LinkedIn users had even more: an average of 786 contacts. See Keith Hampton, Lauren Sessions Goulet, Lee Raine, and Kristin Purcell, "Social Networking and Our Lives," Pew Research Center's *Internet & American Life Project*, June 16, 2011, http://pewinternet.org/Reports/2011/Technology-and-social-networks.aspx, pp. 23–24.

2. Heather H. Huhman, "How Super Connectors Are Changing the Tech World," June 6, 2013, http://tech.co/how-super-connectors-are-changing-the-tech-world-2013-06.

3. Mark Granovetter, *Getting a Job: A Study of Contacts and Careers,* 2nd ed. (Chicago: University of Chicago Press, 1974, 1995), p. 22.

4. Mark Granovetter, "The Strength of Weak Ties: A Network Theory Revisited," *Sociological Theory,* vol. 1 (1983): 201–233; all quotations from p. 202.

5. Noam Wasserman, "Surprising Facts from *The Founder's Dilemmas: Anticipating and Avoiding the Pitfalls That Can Sink a Startup,*" April 4, 2012, http://www.kauffman.org/~/media/kauffman_org/resources/founders_dilemmas_surprising_facts.pdf. *The Founder's Dilemmas* is part of the Kauffman Foundation Series on Innovation and Entrepreneurship.

6. Kevin Dutton, *The Wisdom of Psychopaths: What Saints, Spies, and Serial Killers Can Teach Us About Success* (New York: Scientific American/Farrar, Strauss, and Giroux, 2012), p. 162.

7. Scott O. Lilienfeld and Hal Arkowitz, "What 'Psychopath' Means," *Scientific American,* November 28, 2007, http://www.scientificamerican.com/article.cfm?id=what-psychopath-means.

Chapter 3

1. A. J. Bahns, K. M. Pickett, and C. S. Crandall, "Big Schools, Small Schools and Social Relationships," *Group Processes & Intergroup Relations,* vol. 15, no. 1 (2012): 119–131.

2. Maria Popova, "The Filter Bubble: Algorithm vs. Curator & the Value of Serendipity," interview with Eli Pariser, May 12, 2011, http://www.brainpickings.org/index.php/2011/05/12/the-filter-bubble/.

3. Ibid.

4. Martin Ruef, "Strong Ties, Weak Ties and Islands: Structural and Cultural Predictors of Organizational Innovation," *Industrial and Corporate Change,* vol. 11, no. 3 (2002): 427–449.

5. Bahns, Pickett, and Crandall, "Big Schools, Small Schools."

6. Jeanne Meister, "The Boomer-Millennial Workplace Clash: Is It Real?" *Forbes,* June 4, 2013, http://www.forbes.com/sites/jeannemeister/2013/06/04/the-boomer-millennial-workplace-clash-is-it-real/.

7. The "six degrees of separation" still holds up today. A 2008 study conducted by Microsoft examined records of 30 billion instant messages among 180 million people in different countries in 2006. The researchers looked at how many links it would take to connect 180 billion different pairs of users

of Microsoft Messenger. They found that the average length was 6.6 links and that 78 percent of the pairs could be connected in seven steps or fewer. See Jure Leskovec and Eric Horvitz, "Planetary-Scale Views on an Instant-Messaging Network," *Microsoft Research Technical Report MSR-TR-2006-186*, June 2007.

8. http://www.85broads.com.

Chapter 4

1. Adam Grant, *Give and Take: A Revolutionary Approach to Success* (New York: Penguin, 2013), p. 42.

2. I encountered this story in Brian Uzzi and Shannon Dunlap, "How to Build Your Network," *Harvard Business Review*, vol. 83, no. 12 (December 2005): 53–60, 151.

Chapter 5

1. Susan Cain, *Quiet: The Power of Introverts in a World That Can't Stop Talking* (New York: Crown, 2012), pp. 3, 55.

2. Thomas Gilovich, Victoria Husted Medvec, and Kenneth Savitsky, "The Spotlight Effect in Social Judgment: An Egocentric Bias in Estimations of the Salience of One's Own Actions and Appearance," *Journal of Personality and Social Psychology*, vol. 78, no. 2 (2000): 211–222.

3. James Pennebaker, *Opening Up: The Healing Power of Expressing Emotions* (New York: Guilford, 1997), p. 3.

4. According to a 1999 study by the National Center for Missing & Exploited Children, it was estimated that more than 200,000 children were abducted by family members, while 58,000 were abducted by nonfamily members (no indication of whether the nonfamily member abductors were friends or acquaintances of the child's family): http://www.missingkids.com/KeyFacts. According to the American Psychological Association, only 10 percent of the perpetrators of child sexual abuse are unknown to the child. See http://www. apa.org/pi/families/resources/child-sexual-abuse.aspx.

5. Ipsos Observer, *Business Card/Networking Study*, prepared for Moo.com, August 2012. Study results described by Teresa Novellino, "Small Biz Prefers In-Person Schmoozing," September 19, 2012, http://upstart.bizjournals.com/news/wire/2012/09/19/small-biz-prefers-in-person-schmoozing.html?ana= e_ubj.

6. Nilofer Merchant, "3 Ways to Fuel Your Own Growth," *Entrepreneurship* blog, May 17, 2013, http://nilofermerchant.com/2013/05/17/3-ways-to-fuel-your-own-growth/.

7. See Richard D. Arvey, Maria Rotundo, Wendy Johnson, Zhen Zhang, and Matt McGue, "The Determinants of Leadership Role Occupancy: Genetic and Personality Factors," *The Leadership Quarterly*, vol. 17 (2006), 1–20. The scientists studied identical and fraternal twins to determine how much of leadership could be determined by genetics, and how much was likely to be the product of environment. A newer study (also of twins) puts the percentage of leadership ability due to genetics at 24 percent; see Jan-Emmanuel De Neve, Slava Mikhaylov, Christopher T. Dawes, Nicholas A. Christakis, and James H. Fowler, "Born to Lead? A Twin Design and Genetic Association Study of Leadership Role Occupancy," *The Leadership Quarterly*, vol. 24 (2013), 45–60.

8. Susan T. Fiske, Amy J. C. Cuddy, and Peter Glick, "Universal Dimensions of Social Cognition: Warmth and Competence," *Trends in Cognitive Sciences*, vol. 11, no. 2 (2007): 77–83.

9. Mark E. McKinney and Amber Benson, "The Value of Brand Trust," *Journal of Brand Strategy*, vol. 2, no. 1 (2013): 76–86.

Chapter 6

1. See Sarah Cliffe, "The Uses and Abuses of Influence: An Interview with Robert Cialdini," *Harvard Business Review*, July 2013, http://hbr.org/2013/07/the-uses-and-abuses-of-influence/ar/1.

2. Martin Zwilling, "Great Entrepreneurs Build Deep People Connections," *Forbes*, February 3, 2013, http://www.forbes.com/sites/martinzwilling/2013/02/03/great-entrepreneurs-build-deep-people-connections/.

3. Samuel López De Victoria, PhD, "The Johari Window," 2008, http://psychcentral.com/blog/archives/2008/07/08/the-johari-window/.

4. Laura Leist, *Eliminate the Chaos at Work: 25 Techniques to Increase Productivity* (New York: Wiley, 2011), p. 13.

5. Nicholas A. Christakis and James H. Fowler, *Connected: The Surprising Power of Our Social Networks and How They Shape Our Lives* (New York: Hachette Book Group, 2009), p. 34.

Chapter 7

1. Susan Cain, *Quiet: The Power of Introverts in a World That Can't Stop Talking* (New York: Crown, 2012), p. 6.

2. Bob Garfield and Doug Levy, *Can't Buy Me Like: How Authentic Customer Connections Drive Superior Results* (New York: Portfolio, 2013), p. 2.

3. Jay Allen, "Accessing the CXO: A Rainmaker's Guide to Building, Managing, and Leveraging Influential Relationships" (unpublished manuscript, 2013), p. 30.

4. Jennifer McCrea and Jeffrey C. Walker, with Karl Weber, *The Generosity Network: New Transformational Tools for Successful Fund-Raising* (New York: Deepak Chopra Books, 2013), pp. 173–174.

5. Adam Grant, *Give and Take: A Revolutionary Approach to Success* (New York: Penguin, 2013), p. 151.

6. Tomi T. Ahonen, *The Annual Mobile Industry Numbers and Stats Blog*, summarizes the findings from the 2013 edition of the *Tomi Ahonen Almanac*, March 6, 2013, http://communities-dominate.blogs.com/brands/2013/03/the-annual-mobile-industry-numbers-and-stats-blog-yep-this-year-we-will-hit-the-mobile-moment.html.

7. A study by the Keller Fay Group discovered that "only 5 percent of our conversations are with acquaintances, and only 2 percent are with strangers." Cited in Paul Adams, *Grouped: How Small Groups of Friends Are the Key to Influence on the Social Web* (Berkeley, CA: New Riders Press, 2012), p. 23.

8. Research reported by the Associated Press, April 28, 2013. Source: http://www.statisticbrain.com/attention-span-statistics/.

9. Graham D. Brodie, "Listening as Positive Communication," in T. Socha and M. Pitts (eds.), *The Positive Side of Interpersonal Communication* (New York: Peter Lang, 2012), pp. 109–110.

10. McCrea and Walker, *The Generosity Network*, p. 169.

11. Stuart Wolpert, "How the Brain Creates the 'Buzz' That Helps Ideas Spread," University of California Los Angeles Newsroom press release, July 5, 2013, http://newsroom.ucla.edu/portal/ucla/how-the-brain-creates-buzz-247204.aspx.

12. Martin Zwilling, "Great Entrepreneurs Build Deep People Connections," *Forbes* online, February 2, 2013, http://www.forbes.com/sites/martinzwilling/2013/02/03/great-entrepreneurs-build-deep-people-connections/.

Chapter 8

1. Neil Patel, "The Two Reasons You Aren't Making Over $100K a Year," *Quick Sprout* blog, May 9, 2013, http://www.quicksprout.com/2013/05/09/the-2-reasons-why-you-arent-making-over-100k-a-year/?utm_source=feedburner&utm_medium=email&utm_campaign=Feed%3A+Quicksprout+%28Quick+Sprout%29.

2. Anthony K. Tjan, Richard J. Harrington, and Tsun-Yan Hiseh, *Heart, Smarts, Guts, and Luck: What It Takes to Be an Entrepreneur and Build a Great Business* (Boston: Harvard Business School Publishing, 2012), p. 62.

3. See Adam Grant, *Give and Take: A Revolutionary Approach to Success* (New York: Penguin, 2013), pp. 40–60.

4. Paul C. Brunson, "It's Called 'Networking,' Not 'Using,'" June 11, 2013, http://paulcbrunson.com/2013/06/its-called-networking-not-using/.

Chapter 9

1. The concept of collaboration producing greater value is drawn from Navi Radjou, Jaideep Prabhu, Prasad Kaipa, and Simone Ahuja, "The New Arithmetic of Collaboration," *Harvard Business Review, HBR Blog Network*, November 4, 2010, http://blogs.hbr.org/2010/11/the-new-arithmetic-of-collabor/.

2. Robyn Scott, "Why a Christmas Experiment in Gratitude Became a Startup," updated August 6, 2013, https://medium.com/editors-picks/a0c2ad69b70d.

3. Richard Koch and Greg Lockwood, *Superconnect: Harnessing the Power of Networks and the Strength of Weak Ties* (New York: Norton, 2010), p. 24.

4. Lisa Curtis, "How to Crowdfund $50,000 in Your Spare Time," *Forbes* online, October 1, 2013, http://www.forbes.com/sites/85broads/2013/10/01/how-to-crowdfund-50000-in-your-spare-time/2/.

5. Nicole Carter, "What the Most Successful People Have in Common," *Inc. 5000*, October 12, 2013, http://www.inc.com/nicole-carter/lewis-schiff-what-the-most-successful-people-have-in-common.html.

6. For a concise explanation of Metcalfe's law and social networks, see Michael Simmons, "The Surprising Science Behind How Super Connectors Scale Their Networks," *Forbes Entrepreneur* blog, September 4, 2013, http://www.forbes.com/sites/michaelsimmons/2013/09/04/the-science-behind-how-super-connectors-scale-their-networks/.

7. Nicholas A. Christakis and James H. Fowler, *Connected: The Surprising Power of Our Social Networks and How They Shape Our Lives* (New York: Little, Brown, 2009), p. 20.

Chapter 10

1. I'd like to thank my friend and social media expert Jennifer Abernethy for her input to this chapter.

2. Ipsos Observer, *Business Card/Networking Survey*, August 2012, © 2012 Ipsos, http://us.moo.com/bit-bucket/survey.pdf, p. 7.

3. Lars Backstrom, Paolo Boldi, Marco Rosa, Johan Ugander, and Sebastiano Vigna, "Four Degrees of Separation," January 6, 2012, http://arxiv.org/pdf/1111.4570.pdf.

4. Facebook, LinkedIn, and Twitter numbers from Digital Marketing Ramblings (DMR) website article by Craig Smith, "How Many People Use 370 of the Top Social Media, Apps & Tools?" accessed January 29, 2014, http://

expandedramblings.com/index.php/resource-how-many-people-use-the-top-social-media/. Google+ number from Matt McGee, "Google+ Hits 300 Million Active Monthly 'In-Stream' Users, 540 Million Across Google," October 29, 2013, http://marketingland.com/google-hits-300-million-active-monthly-in-stream-users-540-million-across-google-63354.

5. Richard Branson, "Richard Branson on How to Make the Most of Your Network," *Entrepreneur,* November 4, 2013, http://entrepreneur.com/article/229741#ixzz2jsaCzH5p.

6. The average household income of a LinkedIn member in 2013 was $83,000. See Devon Glenn, "Are You Wealthier Than the Average LinkedIn User," *Social Times*, May 7, 2013, http://socialtimes.com/linkedin-user-statistics-affluent-educated-influential_b126197.

7. Wayne Breitbarth, Portrait of a LinkedIn User, 2013 Edition, infographic, July 2013, http://www.powerformula.net/misc/linkedin-infographic-portrait-of-a-linkedin-user-2013.html.

8. Ibid.

9. Jaime Tardy, "7 Ways I Got to Know Over 100 Millionaires and How You Can Get to Know Them Too," *Quick Sprout*, November 4, 2013, http://www.quicksprout.com/2013/11/04/7-ways-i-got-to-know-over-100-millionaires-and-how-you-can-get-to-know-them-too/.

10. Wayne Breitbarth, "Need Help Capitalizing on Networking Events? LinkedIn to the Rescue!" *Power Formula LinkedIn Blog*, November 3, 2013, http://www.powerformula.net/?p=3376&option=com_wordpress&Itemid=17.

11. Paul Ingram and Michael W. Morris, "Do People Mix at Mixers? Structure, Homophily, and the 'Life of the Party,'" *Administrative Science Quarterly*, vol. 52, no. 4 (December 2007): 558–585.

Chapter 11

1. Kay Koplovitz, "Women & Augusta: The Long Drive from the First Tee to the Green Jacket," *Kay's blog*, April 6, 2012, http://koplovitz.com/women-augusta-the-long-drive-from-the-first-tee-to-the-green-jacket/.

2. Sheryl Sandberg, *Lean In: Women, Work, and the Will to Lead* (New York: Knopf, 2013), p. 7.

3. Source: Catalyst Knowledge Center, *Pyramid: U.S. Women in Business* (New York: Catalyst, 2013), http://www.catalyst.org/knowledge/us-women-business-0. In finance, women do better in some circumstances and worse in others. We are 15.9 percent of the executive officers and 19.3 percent of the board directors. But, according to Catalyst, in 2013 no CEO of a financial company was a woman. Source: Catalyst Knowledge Center, *Pyramid: Women in U.S. Finance* (New York: Catalyst, 2013), http://www.catalyst.org/knowledge/women-us-finance-0.

4. Cristian L. Dezso and David Gaddis Ross, *Does Female Representation in Top Management Improve Firm Performance? A Panel Data Investigation.* Robert H. Smith School Research Paper No. RHS 06-104, March 9, 2011. Available at SSRN: http://ssrn.com/abstract=1088182.

5. Nancy M. Carter and Harvey M. Wagner, contributors, *The Bottom Line: Corporate Performance and Women's Representation on Boards (2004–2008),* March 1, 2011 (New York: Catalyst, 2011), The_Bottom_Line_Corporate_Performance_and_Womens_Representation_on_Boards.pdf.

6. Athena Vongalis-Macrow writes, "Many networking opportunities are organized around male interests. The male-centeredness of networking means that making connections to get ahead continues to be an issue for many women seeking to progress their careers." "Two Ways Women Can Network More Effectively, Based on Research," *Harvard Business Review* blog, November 26, 2012, http://blogs.hbr.org/2012/11/two-ways-women-can-network-more/.

7. Catalyst, *The Double Bind Dilemma for Women in Leadership: Damned If You Do, Doomed If You Don't,* Catalyst Publication Code D68, 2007, p. 8. http://www.catalyst.org/knowledge/double-bind-dilemma-women-leadership-damned-if-you-do-doomed-if-you-dont-0.

8. For an analysis of the "likability index" of men and women throughout their business careers, see Jack Zenger and Joseph Folkman's article, "New Research Shows Success Doesn't Make Women Less Likable," *Harvard Business Review* blog, April 4, 2013, http://blogs.hbr.org/2013/04/leaning-in-without-hesitation/.

9. This study is cited in Kay Koplovitz's article "The 'Women' Effect: Women Have More Influence on Men's Behavior Than Previously Thought, and It's Changing Corporate America," *Huffington Post,* July 23, 2103, http://www.huffingtonpost.com/kay-koplovitz/the-women-effect_b_3636468.html.

10. This study was cited in Adam Grant, *Give and Take: A Revolutionary Approach to Success* (New York: Penguin, 2013), p. 208.

11. Sarah Cliffe, "The Uses (and Abuses) of Influence: An Interview with Robert Cialdini," *Harvard Business Review,* July 2013, http://hbr.org/2013/07/the-uses-and-abuses-of-influence/ar/1.

12. Hannah Riley Bowles, Linda Babcock, and Kathleen L. McGinn, "Constraints and Triggers: Situational Mechanics of Gender in Negotiation," *Journal of Personality and Social Psychology,* vol. 89 (2005): 951–965. Reported in Adam Grant, *Give and Take: A Revolutionary Approach to Success* (New York: Penguin, 2013), p. 205.

13. Christine Silva and Herminia Ibarra, "Study: Women Get Fewer Game-Changing Leadership Roles," *Harvard Business Review* blog, November 2012, http://blogs.hbr.org/2012/11/study-women-get-fewer-game-changing/.

14. "The Top 10 Workplace Advantages of Being a Woman," *Yahoo! Shine*, October 15, 2012, http://shine.yahoo.com/secrets-to-your-success-20120120/top-10-workplace-advantages-being-woman-135500879.html.

15. Kay Koplovitz, "How Do I Find the Right Mentor?" *Huffington Post*, March 20, 2013, http://www.huffingtonpost.com/kay-koplovitz/mentorship_b_2907929.html.

16. Pamela Ryckman, *Stiletto Network: Inside the Women's Power Circles That Are Changing the Face of Business* (New York: American Management Association [AMACOM], 2013), p. 30.

17. This story was reported in a profile of Abner J. Mikva by John Schwartz, "In a Mentor, Kagan's Critics See Liberal Agenda," *New York Times*, June 25, 2010, http://www.nytimes.com/2010/06/26/us/politics/26mikva.html?_r=0.

18. Athena Vongalis-Macrow, "Two Ways Women Can Network More Effectively, Based on Research," *Harvard Business Review* blog, November 26, 2012, http://blogs.hbr.org/2012/11/two-ways-women-can-network-more/.

19. Linda Babcock and Sara Laschever, *Ask for It: How Women Can Use the Power of Negotiation to Get What They Really Want* (New York: Bantam Dell, 2008), p. 253.

20. Victoria Pynchon, "I Am Woman, Hear Me Network," *Forbes* online, December 30, 2011, http://www.forbes.com/sites/shenegotiates/2011/12/30/i-am-woman-hear-me-network/.

Chapter 12

1. Nathan Heller, "Bay Watched: How San Francisco's New Entrepreneurial Culture Is Changing the Country," *New Yorker*, October 14, 2013, p. 76.

2. Dale Stephens, "A Smart Investor Would Skip the M.B.A.," *Wall Street Journal*, March 1, 2013, http://online.wsj.com/news/articles/SB10001424127887323884304578328243334068564.

3. Ayelet Meron Ruscio, Timothy A. Brown, Wai Tat Chiu, Jitender Sareen, Murray B. Stein, and Ronald C. Kessler, "Social Fears and Social Phobia in the United States: Results from the National Comorbidity Survey Replication," *Psychological Medicine*, vol. 38, no. 1 (January 2008): 15–28, http://www.ncbi.nlm.nih.gov/pmc/articles/PMC2262178/?tool=pubmed.

4. Private interview on November 25, 2013, with Adam Grant, author of *Give and Take: A Revolutionary Approach to Success* (New York: Penguin, 2013).

5. See Adam Grant, "The Peacock and the Panda," *Give and Take: A Revolutionary Approach to Success* (New York: Penguin, 2013), chap. 2, pp. 39–60.

6. Robyn Scott, "Why a Christmas Experiment in Gratitude Became a Startup," August 16, 2013, https://medium.com/editors-picks/a0c2ad69b70d.

7. Private interview on November 25, 2013, with Adam Grant.

8. Susan McPherson and Caroline Howard, "Women Changing the World: Janet Hanson," *Forbes* online, 2012, http://www.forbes.com/special-report/2012/power-women/women-changing-the-world.html.

9. Angie Chang, "This Is What an Angel Investor Looks Like: Meet Angel Investor Janet Hanson," *Women 2.0*, September 5, 2012, http://women2.com/this-is-what-an-angel-investor-looks-like-janet-hanson/.

Resources

While there are many different programs, apps, and resources to help you map your power circles and manage your connections, here are a few that I use and/or recommend as of the writing of this book (2014). You also can download the forms I use to keep track of my connections at http://www. judyrobinett.com/resources.

Mapping Your Power Circles

Laura Leist's Eliminate the Chaos website (http://www.eliminatethechaosat-work.com/) is filled with great information on managing your connections as well as the rest of your life. Her books, including *Eliminate the Chaos at Work: The 25 Techniques to Increase Productivity* (Wiley, 2011), are excellent, especially the information they contain on electronic information management.

Lee Blaylock's Who@ (www.whoat.net) is a "freemium" membership website that connects members privately with other valuable business contacts. It offers a full platform via the Internet including mobile, CRM, and other channels, and it is compatible with Apple, Android, and Windows as well as most e-mail programs including Google's Gmail, Microsoft's Outlook .com, and Yahoo!

Jennifer Abernethy is an expert in social media marketing, and her book *The Complete Idiot's Guide to Social Media Marketing,* Second Edition (New York: Penguin, 2012), is a topnotch guide. I also recommend her website The Sales Lounge (http://www.thesaleslounge.com/) as a resource for keeping up on trends in social media.

Founder and CEO of Pipeline Fellowship, an angel investing "bootcamp" for women, Natalia Oberti Noguera has created Ask & Offer (http://www.askandoffer.co), which creates, screens, and tracks introductions.

Other Software

Contact management. If you use an Apple Mac, iPad, or iPhone, VIPorbit (http://www.viporbit.com/) will help you customize your contact management files and sync them across all of your devices. Evernote (http://evernote.com/) is also a popular contact management program.

Mind mapping. I use mind mapping software to draw my power circles because these programs are excellent in their ability to show links between individuals (instead of ideas). I have used MindMap Creator by GentleSoft, but other popular mind mapping programs include MindJet, XMind, Coggle, and MindNode.

E-mail and marketing software. Infusionsoft and Constant Contact are the industry standards for CRM, sales, and marketing automation.

Index

About the Author

Judy Robinett is a business thought leader who is known as "the woman with the titanium digital Rolodex." She has been profiled in *Forbes, Venture Beat, Huffington Post,* and *Bloomberg Businessweek* as a sterling example of the new breed of "super connectors" who use their experience and networks to accelerate growth and enhance profitability.

In her more than 30 years of experience as an entrepreneur and corporate leader, Robinett has served as the CEO of both public and private companies and in management positions at Fortune 500 companies. She has been on the advisory boards of Illuminate Ventures, an early-stage venture capital firm based in Menlo Park, California; Pereg Ventures, a venture capital firm based in New York; Springboard Enterprises based in Washington, DC; and Women Innovate Mobile (WIM) accelerators based in New York.

She was the managing director of Golden Seeds Angel Network (the third most active angel investment group and one of the largest in the United States); the CEO of publicly traded Medical Discoveries; and she served on the faculty of Goldman Sachs's 10,000 Small Businesses program.

She was a member of the Department of Commerce team that defined performance criteria for the Malcolm Baldrige National Quality Award for Performance Excellence in Healthcare, for which she received an award from President Bill Clinton.

Robinett has given over 300 speeches worldwide for audiences at MIT, BIO-Europe, CalPoly, AT&T, Westinghouse, and the Department of Energy.

She is the coauthor of a chapter in *Crowdfunding for Dummies* by Sherwood Neiss, Jason W. Best, and Zak Cassady-Dorion (Wiley, 2013).

Robinett lives in Salt Lake City, Utah.

Claim your free bonuses.
Start mining your network today.

Your quick start kit is included with your book purchase. Download it today to get exclusive access to Judy's:

Quick Start Forms

Network Mapping Templates

White Papers

Just scan this QR code:

Or go to: JudyRobinett.com/Resources